GIFTS FOR THE SEEKER

This edition printed and distributed by
Fons Vitae, Louisville, Kentucky

Printed in Canada

Library of Congress Control Number: 2003107314

ISBN-1-887752-57-9

This edition published by
Fons Vitae
49 Mockingbird Valley Dr.
Louisville, KY 40207-1366
fonsvitaeky@aol.com
www.fonsvitae.com

Cover photo: Stephenie Hollyman, ARAMCO World, PADIA

Cover design by Folio.

Gifts for the Seeker

Imam 'Abdallah Ibn 'Alawi Al-Haddad

Revised Edition

Translated from the Arabic by

Mostafa Al-Badawi

FONS VITAE

QUILLIAM

Other Related Fons Vitae Titles

Three Early Sufi Texts:
A Treatise on the Heart
Bayan al-Farq bayn al-Sadr wa-al-Qalb wa-al-Fu'ad wa-al-Lubb
Attributed to Al-Hakim Al-Tirmidhi (D. C. 300/912)
Introduced and Translated by Nicholas Heer

Stations of the Righteous *(Darajat al-sadiqin)* &
The Stumblings of those Aspiring (*Zalal al-fuqara'*):
TwoTexts on the Path of Blame
by Abu 'abd Al-Rahman Al-Sulami Al-Naysaburi (D. 412/1021)
Introduced and Translated by Kenneth L. Honerkamp

Me and Rumi: The Autobiography of Shems-i Tabrizi,
Translated, Introduced and Annotated by William C. Chittick

The Lives of Man–A Guide to the Human States:
Before Life, In the World, and After Death,
by Imam Abdallah Ibn Alawi Al-Haddad, Translated by Mostafa Al-Badawi

The Degrees of the Soul,
by Shaykh Abd Al-Khaliq Al-Shabrawi, Tranlated by Mostafa Al-Badawi

The Book of Assistance,
by Imam Abdallah Alawi Al-Haddad, Translated by Mostafa Al-Badawi

Early Sufi Women,
by Abu Abd ar-Rahman as-Sulami, Translated by Rkia E. Cornell

The Autobiography of a Moroccan Soufi: Ahmad Ibn Ajiba,
Translated by Jean-Louis Michon and from the French by David Streight

Al-Ghazali's Path to Sufism–his Deliverance from Error
al-Munqidh min al-Dalal,
Translated by RJ McCarthy with a Preface by David Burrell
and Introduction by William A. Graham

Al Ghazali **Faith in Divine Unity & Trust in Divine Providence,**
Translated with an Introduction by David B. Burrell

Letters of Sufi Master: The Shaykh ad-Darqawi,
Translated by Titus Burckhardt with a Foreword by Martin Lings

The Name & the Named,
Compiled by Shaykh Tosun Bayrak al-Jerrahi al-Halveti
with a Foreword by William C. Chittick

Ibn Arabi **Divine Governance of the Human Kingdom,**
Interpreted by Shaykh Tosun Bayrak al-Jerrahi al-Halveti

Suhrawardi **The Shape of Light,**
Interpreted by Shaykh Tosun Bayrak al-Jerrahi al-Halveti

CONTENTS

TRANSLATOR'S INTRODUCTION

Tawḥīd, or 'Unification', is the central doctrine of Islam: the affirmation of the Divine unity, omnipotence, and utter transcendence. Of necessity, it is presented in the Qur'ān in a form accessible to all Muslims, since there exists a certain minimum of knowledge which must reach every member of our Community. However, behind this outward shell can be discerned layer within layer of ever-deepening meaning, each level being closed to all but those who possess the necessary spiritual qualifications.

Tawḥīd possesses two main strata: the exoteric or outermost dimension, to be apprehended rationally, which is the domain of the theologian (*mutakallim*); and the esoteric, or inner dimension, which is that of the Sufi. The latter is again divided into two parts, each of which comprises innumerable degrees. The first of these consists of everything that can be expressed symbolically, whether through verbal or any other means of communication. This is the domain of the seeker (*murīd*), who must embark on an intensive programme of self-purification if he is to liberate the heart and transform it into a receptacle of inspiration and spiritual sight. The second consists of that which is by its very nature inexpressible, and cannot therefore be obtained secondhand: it is to be realized directly by spiritual contemplation (*mushāhada*), and is the exclusive domain of the *ʿārif bi'llāh*, whom in English we term the 'gnostic'.

The author of this book was the venerable Imām ʿAbdallāh al-Ḥaddād, who died at Tarīm in the Ḥaḍramawt valley in South Arabia, and was regarded as the undisputed master of his time in both exoteric knowledge and gnosis. He was the *barzakh*, or connecting isthmus, between the two oceans, that of *sharīʿa*, or outward knowledge, and *ḥaqīqa*: knowledge attained through immediate and direct vision.

'Sufism', as the generic term for the inner aspects of Islam, is firstly doctrine, then method, and finally realization. This small work, dictated as a response to a number of questions submitted to the Imām by a man who was already himself of considerable spiritual rank, contains elements of all three dimensions. It begins with a brief but lucid exposition of the doctrine of Unification in the exoteric manner, followed by a clarification of various questions of spiritual method and experience, and concludes with what is the most important part of the book: a commentary on a poem of gnosis written by one of the greatest knowers of God ever produced by the Bā-ʿAlawī Sayyids, Imām Abū Bakr al-ʿAydarūs of Aden.

This is a book which repays thoughtful and repeated attention. New dimensions appear with each new reading, and these can be assimilated with the benefit of meditation and the maturity brought about by the passage of time. As with our other translations of Imām al-Ḥaddād's writings, we have depended on the explanations and support of Ḥabīb Aḥmad Mashhūr al-Ḥaddād.

It is to be hoped that our efforts at making the wisdom of Imām al-Ḥaddād accessible to English-speaking readers will make a useful contribution to the battle against the anti-spiritual trend of the new 'Age of Ignorance'. At a time when the very criteria which allowed men to distinguish between reality and illusion are being lost, when truth is submerged under a massive output of trivial and distracting, if not outrightly diabolical material masquerading as knowledge, we believe the publication of works such as this to be an urgent necessity.

I am indebted to Abdal-Hakim Murad for translating all the poetry contained in this volume, as well as for revising the text. The subdivisions and chapter titles are ours. Quotations from the Holy Qur'ān are based on the translations of Arberry and Pickthall.

We trust that in the infinitude of His grace, God shall overlook our shortcomings, and accept our endeavour.

MOSTAFA AL-BADAWI,
al-Madina al-Munawwara,
Rajab, 1410

GIFTS FOR THE SEEKER, *being* SOME ANSWERED QUESTIONS

Prologue

In the name of God, the Merciful and Compassionate

No power is there, and no strength, but by God, the High, the Great!

Transcendent are You! We have no knowledge save that which You have taught us. You are indeed the Knowing, the Wise! [2:32]

All praise belongs to God, Who never disappoints those who hope in Him, never refuses those who ask of Him, never ignores those who quest for Him, never underpays those who act for Him, never deprives those who thank Him, never fails those who battle for Him, never allows those whose comfort is in His remembrance to be estranged, never surrenders to others those who surrender to His might, never abandons to others those who depend on Him, and never forsakes those who trust and commit themselves to Him. Those who firmly hold to His Book shall never err, and those who take refuge in His Presence shall never find disgrace.

I praise Him for all that He has inspired and taught, and thank Him for all His grace and bounties. His help I request to fulfil His immense right [upon us], and I seek refuge in the light of His noble Countenance against the loss of His favours and the onslaught of affliction. It is God I ask to whelm with His blessings and peace His most noble Prophet, most eminent Messenger and greatest Beloved, who is our master and patron Muḥammad, and his Family and Companions, who are the essence of excellence and generosity, the very fountainhead of knowledge and wisdom. And may these blessings and peace endure for as long as pens write and banners are unfurled!

To proceed. The righteous shaykh of integrity and intelligent understanding, ʿAbd al-Raḥmān ibn ʿAbdallāh ʿAbbād, has requested me to answer a number of questions which he committed to writing and presented to me in the town of Shibām after my visit to the great gnostic shaykh Saʿīd ibn ʿĪsā al-ʿAmūdī,[1] and to other people of virtue, both living and dead, in those regions. I perceived in him signs of eagerness for the truth, combined with the fragrance of sincerity, and therefore promised him a response. The time has now come to fulfil that promise—by God's ability and power—and to welcome the arrival of his pertinent questions with the hospitable offer of clear replies.

I feel it is appropriate to precede these answers with a prologue which will give insight and reassurance both to the questioner, and to all other intelligent people of similar tendency.

Therefore I seek God's help, relying on Him, committing myself to Him, and asking Him (Transcendent is He!) to guide me to that which is correct in His sight, for He *guides whom He will to a straight Path* [10:25]; *the path of God to Whom belongs all that is in the heavens and the earth. Indeed, to God do all things return.* [42:53]

I say: Know that to put a question whenever a need or a problem arises and to seek further knowledge and insight is the wont and custom of the élite of every time and place. It is deemed obligatory where obligatory knowledge is concerned, and a virtue in the case of supererogatory knowledge. For questions are the keys to the sciences and the secrets of the Unseen which some people carry in their hearts and breasts. Just as valuables and goods kept within locked houses can be reached only by using keys fashioned of iron or wood, so too are these sciences and gnoses, borne by scholars and gnostics, to be reached only by questions fashioned out of the wish to profit, and accompanied by sincerity, enthusiasm, and courteous manners. Questioning is encouraged and enjoined by the *Sharīʿa*, for God the Exalted has said: *Ask those who recite the Book before you*, [10:94] and *Ask the people of remembrance if you do not know; with the clear signs and the Scriptures.* [16:43–4] And the Messenger of God, may blessings and peace be upon him, has said: 'A good question is [already] half of knowledge.' The intention of every leading scholar or Imām who has ever informed others of the breadth of his knowledge was that this should be known about him so that people might ask and seek it from him. This was related in the case of ʿAlī,[2] may God ennoble his face, Ibn Masʿūd,[3] Ibn ʿAbbās,[4] Ibn ʿUmar,[5] Abū Hurayra,[6] and others among our [early] predecessors and those who came later, may God be pleased with them all. And there were other scholars, such as ʿUrwa ibn al-Zubayr,[7] al-Ḥasan al-Baṣrī[8] and Qatāda,[9] who likewise encouraged people to put questions to them. Sufyān al-Thawrī[10] immediately left any town he entered when none of its people asked him for knowledge, saying: 'This is a town where knowledge dies'. Whenever al-Shiblī,[11] may God have mercy on him, sat in his [teaching] circle and no questions were put forth to him, he would recite: *'And the word shall fall upon them because of their wrongdoing; they do not speak.'* [27:85]

A scholar may sometimes question his companions to assess their knowledge and so be able to benefit them. It has been related in a sound *ḥadīth* that the Messenger of God, may blessings and peace be upon him, once asked a group of his Companions about a tree the leaves of which did not fall and which resembled the believer. None of those present answered, so he informed them, may blessings and peace be upon him, that it was the date-palm. Ibn ʿUmar[5] was there, and had recognised it, but kept his silence; when subsequently he informed his father the latter blamed him for his silence. ʿUmar,[12] may God be pleased with him, often questioned his companions, and whenever one of them replied, 'God knows best,' he would become angry, and declare: 'I did not ask you about God's knowledge, but about yours: either say "I know" or "I know not"!'

A scholar may question one of his companions about something which he already knows, so that others present may benefit. Such, for example, were the questions put to the Messenger of God, may blessings and peace be upon him, by Gabriel, peace be upon him, concerning Islam, *Īmān* and *Iḥsān*.[13]

A lesser man may for subtle reasons be in possession of a particular item of knowledge unknown to a superior one, and the latter may thus need to ask him about it. An example of this is ʿUmar's questioning of Ḥudhayfa,[14] may God be pleased with them, about [future] tribulations, and about the hypocrites.

A scholar may ask his equal, or one who is nearly so, about the way he has understood certain things in God's Book and the *Sunna* of His Messenger, may blessings and peace be upon him, to see whether they share the same opinion, which will serve to confirm or strengthen it. This again resembles the practice of ʿUmar, may God be pleased with him, who asked a group of the Companions about a particular interpretation of the verse *When support comes from God, and victory*, [110:1] and only Ibn ʿAbbās agreed with him—may God be pleased with them both.[15] Many such things occurred with great men, in both the early and later [generations]. As for ʿUmar's question to ʿAlī, may God be pleased with them both, the purpose behind it was to learn from him, since ʿAlī was granted a privilege shared by no other Companion, which was to be the 'Gate to the City of Knowledge'—the city being the Messenger himself, may blessings and peace be upon him.[16] As for the order given by the Messenger of God to his Companions not to ask him too many questions, this prohibition, although stated in general terms, was particularly directed at questions concerning legal judgements, retaliatory punishments [*qiṣāṣ*] or *ḥudūd*[17] and public affairs. This was out of compassion for the Nation, and out of the merciful wish that they should not be charged with something they would be unable to implement. The evidence to support this is His saying, *O you who believe! Inquire not after things which, if they were discovered to you, would vex you, yet if you question concerning them when the Qur'ān is being sent down, they will be discovered to you. God has effaced those things, for God is Forgiving, Forbearing. A people before you questioned concerning them, then disbelieved in them.* [5:101–2] And there is also the saying of the Messenger of God, may blessings and peace be upon him: 'God has made certain obligations incumbent upon you; so neglect them not. He has drawn limits; therefore violate them not. He has prohibited certain things, therefore commit them not. And He has remained silent concerning certain things—out of mercy for you, not out of forgetfulness—therefore do not inquire about them.' And in another *ḥadīth*: 'Those who came before you were destroyed by their great inquisitiveness and their arguments about [what was brought to them by] their Prophets.' A man once asked the Messenger of God, upon whom be blessings and peace, whether the Pilgrimage [*ḥajj*] was a yearly obligation, and the Prophet kept his silence. When he repeated his question, he replied: 'Once in a lifetime; and had I said "Yes!" it would have become obligatory for you, and you would have been unable to comply.' Underlying this anecdote is a noble secret which it is not permissible to disclose in writing, but you can search for it within the context of His saying (Exalted is He!): *Whoever obeys the Messenger has obeyed God,* [4:80] and *Those who pledge their allegiance to you do but pledge their allegiance to God.* [48:10]

A disciple who asks his shaykh a question, or a student who asks his teacher, should have no other aim but to benefit, and should beware of wanting to test him, for that may lead to his deprivation and failure. When a disciple or student asks a shaykh or a scholar about something the knowledge of which may be harmful or beyond his understanding, then the latter should stop and ponder; they are to inform the questioner of his lack of qualification only if their assessment of him is that [such a response] will not break his heart, and be religiously damaging to him, or that no aversion will arise in his soul which would deflect him from his quest; otherwise they should stoop in their answer to his level of knowledge and understanding.

Should they divert the answer from the strict implication of the question they are not to say, as one of the people of realization once said:

> It is my duty to carve rhymes from the bedrock of words;
> It is not my concern if cattle do not comprehend.

For such an utterance is peculiar to a certain spiritual state and situation.

A shaykh or a scholar is like a compassionate father and a gentle tutor; he speaks in such a manner as to be of benefit and profit. Gnostics, however, are subject to overpowering and absorbing spiritual states in which they become unable to keep in mind what we have just mentioned; their states should be concedingly ackowledged, for they are too high in rank to be objected to or accused of ignorance or negligence. This is not the place, moreover, to elaborate a justification of such authoritative writers for divulging in their books and treatises the secrets of Lordship and the realities of the Unseen.

It may be permissible for a man to question another with the intention of testing him in two situations. The first is when a scholar, compassionate and of good counsel, sees a man so deeply under the sway of self-admiration that he is prevented from seeking knowledge, or from adding to the knowledge which he already has, or from acknowledging the merits of the virtuous; he may then question him—preferably in private—to test and try him, so that this man may know his real worth, this being a form of counsel to him. The second is when one sees a hypocrite speaking assertively, and threatening to confuse weak believers by introducing into religion things which do not belong to it; he may then question him in their presence to test him and demonstrate to them his failings and his ignorance. While doing so, his intention should be to counsel and warn him about his faults, in the hope that he will return to a fairer judgement and submit to the truth. It is this that has drawn the scholars, may God be pleased with them, into debates with those who innovate, deviate, or falsify the truth.

Whenever a scholar is asked for information which he ought to be teaching, it is not permissible for him to keep silent, for the Prophet has said (upon him be blessings and peace): 'On the Day of Rising, God will garb in a bridle of fire the man who withholds knowledge that is requested of him.'

The scholars of the present time must not keep their knowledge to themselves and wait for someone to come along and ask, for most people today are complacent about religion, uninterested in knowledge and in anything else that will benefit them in the hereafter, to the extent that a man's beard may grow white and he still knows nothing of the obligatory parts of the ritual ablution and prayer, or what is mandatory for him to know by way of belief in God, His Angels, Books, Messengers and the Last Day. The very states of such people mutely proclaim their ignorance; and for scholars endowed with understanding, that is sufficient to be a question.

A seeker travelling to God, whose sole aim is to acquire knowledge of Him, and whose wish is to rid himself of anything that may distract him from going to Him, should never ask for knowledge unless it is necessary in his [own particular] state and time. However, in this blessed time of ours, such a seeker is stranger than the Phoenix and rarer than the philosopher's stone. So let each man be prolific in his questioning after knowledge, so as to profit and grow, for a believer is never sated with good things. In a *ḥadīth* it is said: 'Two [kinds of] people can never get enough: those who are avid for knowledge, and those who are avid for money.' The proof for what we have just said about the seeker is what is related about Dawūd al-Ṭā'ī,[18] may God's mercy be upon him. When he decided to devote himself to God he began by sitting with the scholars: he thus kept the company of Imām Abū Ḥanīfa,[19] may God's mercy be upon him, for nearly a year. Sometimes, when a question arose [in his mind] which he was, in his own words: 'more eager to know than a thirsting man is eager for cool water,' he refrained from asking about it, the reason being, as we said earlier, that a seeker is only to ask about that which is a necessity for him.

There are many proofs for the correctness of the topics discussed in this brief introduction; and it would lead us away from our intended brevity if we were to delve into every one of them. The indications that we have given will, however, be sufficient.

Success is from God, also help and confirmation. We trust in Him, upon Him do we rely. He is our sufficiency, and He is Best of Custodians.

It is now time to begin fulfilling our purpose. *God speaks the truth, and He guides to the way.* [33:4]

THE FIRST RESPONSE

On the meanings of Lā ilāha illa'Llāh

(a) Introduction to the Science of Unification

You ask—may God honour you with enlightened understanding, and with the Opening of Lordship [*al-fatḥ al-rabbānī*][20]—about the meaning of *Lā ilāha illa'Llāh*. Know that all the religious knowledges and practical measures are but unfoldings of the meaning of this noble phrase and of the rights it has [over mankind], which take the form of injunctions, prohibitions, promises, warnings, and their entailments. That which is an exposition of its rights is consequently an explanation of it. The purpose [of this statement] is to make you aware that it is impossible to know fully the details of [each of] its sciences, let alone write them all down, as [will become evident] from what is to follow.

To explain what it means in itself: it is the knowledge termed the 'Science of Unification' [*ʿilm al-tawḥīd*], which is a teeming sea the shore of which can never be reached and the bottom never fathomed. The theologians [*mutakallimūn*] have skimmed over its vast surface, while the realizing gnostics have plunged into its depths and attained to some of its precious and innumerable subtleties, gems, and wonderful and strange things. Following their prolonged and profound search, and having exhausted their energies and abilities, they unanimously confessed their inability to reach its limit or perceive its end. This was because in order fully to apprehend the science of Unification, one has fully to apprehend the Essence and Attributes of the Unified—and He is immeasurably too high for that. All sound authorities are agreed that fully to apprehend the Essence and Attributes of God the Exalted is impossible, whether in this world or the next. The man belonging to the Faction [*ṭā'ifa*][21] who gave the impression that it could occur was an exception. There is no need to mention his name, since the error of his position is evident. Fully to apprehend Him is impossible because it would require a certain mastery and power to seize; for someone who 'apprehends' something, whether by knowing everything about it, or in any other manner, is seizing and mastering it, partly or fully, whereas the Real (Exalted is He!), is the Master, Who cannot be mastered. Know this!

There are two parts to the science of Unification. The first part is outward, to be learned through arguments and proofs. It is a duty for every believer to know a certain minimum amount of this, without which his faith will not be sound. A 'theologian' [*mutakallim*] is a man concerned with the exposition and defense of this science, and the enquiry into its arguments and proofs. Although this gives him superiority over the common believers, this superiority must be one of faith and knowledge; otherwise it will be nothing but an empty shell.

The second part is inward; it is that which can only be perceived through Unveiling [*kashf*] and Contemplation [*mushāhada*]. It is the bequest of *taqwā*, and the essence of that right-guidance which is the fruit of self-discipline [*mujāhada*]. It is a secret between the servant and his Lord. Those who possess it may speak about it among themselves, but they are, may God be pleased with them, extremely careful not to divulge it to the unqualified. It was the practice of al-Junayd,[22] may God have mercy upon him, whenever he wished to discourse upon it with his companions, to lock his door and place the key under his thigh. This they do out of compassion for the believers, for anyone who stumbles across this kind of knowledge without being qualified either denies it, and is thus regarded by God as being among those who reject that with which they are unfamiliar, or else will believe it but understand it in a way which differs from its original intention, and thus stumble into error.

Know that this science is hinted at in the writings of the people of realization, such as the *Revival*[23] and the *Nourishment.*[24] Such authors permitted themselves to do this in order to arouse the yearning of sincere seekers, and because in some contexts the benefit to be derived from the science of religious transaction [*muʿāmala*], which it was their purpose to expound, depends on its mention. Otherwise, they have been very reluctant to make any mention of it. Have you not noticed how Imām al-Ghazālī,[25] may God have mercy upon him, whenever he nears these tumultuous seas, remarks: 'Here we shall withhold the pen', or: 'Here is a secret into which we shall not delve', or: 'This belongs to the science of Unveiling [*mukāshafa*], and it is not our purpose to discuss it in the context of the science of religious transactions,' and so on?

As for those Sufis who included some aspects of this knowledge in their books, such as al-Ḥātimī,[26] al-Jīlānī,[27] and others who acted in similar vein, this should either be attributed to their being overpowered—and a man overpowered is excusable—or to their having received a permission—for the man who receives such permission is under an order which he can but obey—and the secret of the permission granted in such matters is itself one that cannot be divulged.

(b) The exoteric meaning of *Lā ilāha illa'Llāh*

In this section we will discuss one part of the outward meaning of *Lā ilāha illa'Llāh*, having already explained why we should keep silent about its inward meaning. We thus say: Know that there is no god other than Him. He is the Necessary Existent by His essence; the Unique, the One, the Able Sovereign, the Living and Sustaining, the Ancient without beginning, the Eternal without end. He has knowledge of all things, and power over all affairs. He does what He will; *nothing resembles Him, and He is the Hearer, the Seer.* [42:11] Holy is He, and Exalted beyond being resembled or equalled, or having a partner or a minister. He is not subject to time, neither is He distracted by one affair away from another; He is neither subject to location nor affected by contingencies. He is absolutely Independent of all things, whatever their nature and however they are envisaged. All that is not Him needs Him in a way so total that it cannot even be conceived to diminish. He has created all creatures, as well as their actions, whether these be good or evil. *Blessed is God, the Best of Creators!* [23:14] *He guides whom He will, and leads whom He will astray;* [35:8] *He gives to whom He will, and withholds from whom He will; He forgives whom He will and chastises whom He will.* [2:284] *He is not questioned about what He does, rather, they are questioned.* [21:23] He created and provided for them, sent down Books and Messengers to guide them, all out of grace and kindness. To confess His unity and obey Him is an obligation upon His servants, transmitted through His Messengers. He is obligated to none, for He is the Possessor and Master of all; none shares sovereignty with Him, and none has any right over Him. His promise to reward those who act well proceeds from His grace, and His warning that He will punish those who act with evil proceeds from His justice. Only the possessor of the abovementioned attributes is Divine; and, as these attributes undoubtedly belong to God (Exalted is He!), and not a single one, let alone them all, can possibly be attributed to any other, God alone is Divine, and no other divinity exists. Those who deny His divinity, or attribute divinity to other than Him, or give Him a partner therein, commit an immense falsehood and are overwhelmed by loss. They are the ones referred to in God's statement (and Mighty is the Speaker!): *We have created for hell many jinn and men; they have hearts with which they do not understand; they have eyes with which they do not see; they have ears with which they do not hear.*

They are like unto the cattle; nay, they are still further astray. Such are the heedless. [7:179]

(c) Polytheism (*shirk*)

Know that this Noble Phrase has two halves: the first is a negation: *lā ilāha*: 'there is no god'; while the second is an affirmation: *illa'Llāh*: 'other than God'. When the negation followed by the affirmation is uttered by someone who empartners no other deity to God, this means that he has denied and refuted the illusion of the polytheists that there may be another divinity, and also means that the essence of Unification that his heart contains will be reinforced; for it is actively strengthened by the repetition of these words. The Messenger of God, may blessings and peace be upon him, said: 'Renew your faith by [saying] *Lā ilāha illa'Llāh.*'

There are subtle and hidden varieties of *shirk*, which are escaped only by gnostics of authority and those people before whom the pure truth stands unveiled by way of actual vision. Some believers may unwittingly fall prey to some of these varieties: they may for instance believe that someone besides God may independantly bring them benefit or preserve them from misfortune. Other attitudes in the same category include avidity for power and love of superiority over others, the love of being unrestrained and independant, passion for social importance and for eminence and praise, both in people's hearts and in their speech. Says a *ḥadīth*: '*Shirk* is more hidden in my nation than the footfalls of ants.' Showing-off was called the 'smaller *Shirk*' by the Prophet, may blessings and peace be upon him. A man may empartner himself or someone else to God and not be aware of it. Believers should therefore do their utmost to guard themselves against these hidden forms of polytheism, just as they guard themselves against the manifest kind. *Shirk* in this sense does not compromise the basis of faith upon which salvation depends, but it does compromise its perfection. We said at the beginning of this section that when denying divinity to any other than God, the monotheist must intend to refute those who are otherwise illusioned, whether they be polytheists or anyone else of similar orientation. We called their false beliefs 'illusions' since they arise from false conceptions and feeble thinking, and indicate that their constitution has become corrupted and their intellect diminished. For otherwise, how can the existence of Him by Whom all things are manifested not be evident to anyone possessed of sight and hearing, let alone one possessed of insight and the [faculty of the] heart? But none can guide those whom God leads astray: such are the people whose *hearing and eyesight are taken away by God, and He left them sightless in the shadows. Deaf, dumb and blind, they shall not return.* [2:18]

O wonder! How can He be disobeyed,
    Or by the thankless have His name denied?
For God in each and every movement made,
    and every stillness, traces that us guide.
In everything a sign is always laid,
    by which His Oneness standeth testified.

A certain gnostic once said: 'A donkey has more knowledge of God than someone who seeks proof of His unity.'

Were it not for our concern for brevity, for reasons that God knows, we would have elaborated on this in such a way as would have taken aback intelligent and perspicacious men. And God is witness to what I say.

(d) On Unification (*tawḥīd*)

Scholars of authority, may God be pleased with them, state that the Divinity is 'He who is rightfully to be worshipped'; and since the One who is rightfully to be worshipped is the one who creates and provides, and since the One who creates and provides for all beings is God the Exalted, He alone is the Divinity; He alone is to be worshipped, and none is to be empartnered to Him.

For the world to have more than one god is an impossibility, as may be known through both reason and revelation. *There is no divinity but God, the August, the Wise.* [3:6] When alluding to this impossibility, namely, that the world may have two gods, the Exalted declares: *Were there gods in them* [heaven and earth] *other than God, they would go to ruin.* [21:22] *God has taken to Himself no son, nor is there any god with Him: for then each god would have left with what he created, and some of them would have risen up over others. Transcendent is God, beyond that which they describe!* [23:91]

No-one ever claimed divinity in empartnerment with God—as did Nimrod and Pharoah (may God's curse be upon them)—nor was it ever claimed for any object, such as a star or a stone, without signs of imperfection, neediness, incapacity and subjugation (which are attributes which inevitably require contingency and servitude) being clearly manifest in both the human beings who claimed it for themselves, and the objects for which it was claimed. It would appear that those who claimed co-divinity with God were driven by a corrupt illusion and a false reasoning that arose when they beheld their own power over certain things. This is indicated in the saying of God the Exalted, in connection with Nimrod's disputation with the Friend [*al-khalīl*] about his Lord: *Abraham said: My Lord is He who gives life and death. And he said: I give life and death!* [2:258] It is said in one of the Qur'ānic commentaries [*tafsīr*] that in order to prove his untenable claim, Nimrod brought two men, executed one of them, and reprieved the other. And there exists a similar text where Pharoah told his people: *O my people, do I not possess the kingdom of Egypt, and these rivers flowing beneath me? Do you not see?* [43:51] It is not unlikely that these two accursed ones were aware of the falsity of their claim, but were driven by arrogance and ingratitude to deny God and claim for themselves that which was not rightfully theirs; and the folly of their followers who submitted to their authority gave them the opportunity to do so. The Exalted God has said of Pharoah: *So he deceived his people and they obeyed him; surely they were a people corrupt.* [43:54] It is said that when the Nile became low, and his people asked him to make it rise for them, he took them out [to its banks], hid himself from their sight, and then began to rub his face in the dust and implore, beseech and pray to God. And God, by His power, made the Nile to flow, that He might further entangle His enemy, and at this Pharoah said to his people: 'It is I who have caused it to flow for you!' This confirms what we have just said; although within these words, again, there are hidden matters which one is not allowed to record in books.

Know that what we have written in these sections overlaps. We have deliberately omitted any mention of the grammatical analysis of the Phrase, its status in the Law and its merit. The former point lies outside our present purpose, while as far as the latter two issues are concerned, it should be a sufficient exposition to say that the lives and wealth of those who reject it are unprotected, and that they shall remain forever in the fire of Hell; whereas a man who lives as a disbeliever for seventy years, for instance, and then utters it with faith, renders his life and wealth sacrosanct, and will slough off his sins and become as pure as the day his mother gave him birth. A servant who meets God the Exalted with as many sins as all the ancient and recent peoples combined, but who does not empartner anything to God, will be forgiven if God wills, or else punished for his sins; but this punishment will be temporary, since none of the people of Unification will remain in hell forever.

In a *ḥadīth* it is said: 'I was commanded to do battle against people until they bear witness that there is no god but God, and that I am the Messenger of God, and establish the Prayer and pay the *Zakāt*. When they do this, they protect from me their lives and their wealth, except for the rights of Islam; and their wage is incumbent upon God.'

And in another *ḥadīth*: 'Whoever has *lā ilāha illa'Llāh* as his last words shall enter the Garden.'

And: 'The people of *lā ilāha illa'Llāh* do not feel estrangement in their graves,[28] or when they are resurrected. It is as though I were beholding them, rising from their graves, shaking the dust from their heads and saying: "*Praised be God, Who did remove sorrow from us; our Lord is indeed Forgiving, Compassionate* and Thankful."'

And: 'A man shall be called, and ninety-nine scrolls containing his sins shall be unfolded before him, each stretching as far as his eye can see; and these are set on the pan of the Scales which contains his evil deeds. The True God then says: "You have a good deed in Our keeping!" A small scroll is then brought to him, on which it is written *Lā ilāha illa'Llāh*. This is cast onto the other pan, and outweighs all the rest combined.'

Shaykh Ibn Aṭā'illāh has mentioned some of the merits of this Phrase in his book *The Key to Success*.[29]

The benefits and advantages which attach to this Phrase, whether yielded in this world or the next, can never be attained by anyone who separates the Two Testimonies, for their status is identical. Those who acquiesce in the Testimony of Unity and deny that of the Messenger do not belong to the people of Unification. But it does no harm to someone who believes in both *tawḥīd* and the Messengership to say *lā ilāha illa'Llāh*, and not immediately follow it up with the testimony of Messengership: he will not miss any of the blessings which attach to this Phrase. Be aware of this!

This subject ramifies into branches and subtleties which would need more than a whole volume if thoroughly pursued; our aim has been only to indicate a few of the meanings of the Phrase of Unification.

(e) *Lā ilāha illa'Llāh* as a formula of *dhikr*

You should know that this phrase is the most comprehensive and profitable of all invocations; the nearest to bringing about the Opening and illumining the heart with the light of God. It is also the most suitable of invocations for all people, since it includes the meanings of all other invocations, such as *al-ḥamdu li'Llāh*,[30] *subḥān Allāh*,[31] and so on. Each believer should, therefore, make it his inseparable *wird*,[32] his constant *dhikr*,[33] without, however, abandoning the other invocations, of each of which he should have a *wird*.

Every human being is either a traveller, an arriver, or a non-traveller, and all three should hold unceasingly to this invocation. Travellers and non-travellers, since they perceive objects and attribute to them an existence of their own—something which may lead to subtle forms of hidden *shirk*—can only expel these from their souls by constantly repeating this phrase. As for the man who has arrived, this invocation is again the most appropriate for him, because although he perceives things by God, and unceasingly summons them to Him, he is not entirely free from perceiving his own self from time to time, and from reprehensible thoughts unworthy of his rank. It has been handed down to us that Abū Bakr al-Ṣiddīq,[34] may God be pleased with him, used to insert this phrase into his conversation: he would utter a few words, say *lā ilāha illa'Llāh*, and then resume what he was saying. This pertains to the Station of Subsistence [*baqā'*] which follows that of Extinction [*fanā'*]. As we said earlier, there is no invocation more appropriate for a man constantly to use than this; however, when the traveller reaches the initial stages of extinction, and is liberated from perceiving any of the worlds [as autonomous], then the most appropriate thing for him at that time is to keep to the Name of Allah. This is what the people of gnosis have advised.

All the above is from the point of view of choosing the best and most appropriate alternative, for otherwise all the invocations are paths leading to God. The shaykhs, may God be pleased with them, have many methods of uttering this honourable Phrase, whether aloud or silently, and have set conditions which the invoker who would expose himself to the Divine effulgence and the Lordly Opening needs to fulfil. These are explained in those of their treatises which deal with them specifically, where they can be found by whoever wishes to tread the path of such men. It is best that those who are able to find in their time a shaykh of authority should receive these from him directly, since books are a last resort for those who are unable to find [such a teacher]; and what a difference there is between a man who receives the Path from a gnostic of authority who will take him to God, and one who only picks it up from a book!

God guides to what is right. To Him is the return, and success is from Him and in His Hand.

THE SECOND RESPONSE

On presence with God

You have asked what 'forcible presence' means. Now, you should firstly know that the original nature of man is to be free of heart, ready to receive whatever comes to him, whether it be that which reforms and enlightens him, or that which brings corruption and darkness. It is the thing which reaches him first which establishes and inscribes itself within him, and he will need to strive and exert himself forcibly to be able to efface it. The first thing to reach the hearts of the children of Adam—except those whom God preserves—is the knowledge of the affairs of their worldly milieu, of the things they do to live and take pleasure therein; these are the first things that they hear and see from their own kind. If, once these things have seized their hearts, there comes to them the knowledge of God and of the rights of Lordship that are His, and they are then requested to fulfil these rights as befits the Holy Presence, they find in their hearts no space for them to dwell and be established; they thus remain shaky and weakly ingrained. The one who aspires for the firm establishment of the knowledge of God in his heart, and for presence with Him during his ordinary activities and in all circumstances to become his custom and sign, will inevitably need to erase the knowledge of worldly affairs that had first entered his heart and which distracts him from devoting himself to this matter and achieving it fully. It is again inevitable that he suffer hardship during his necessary self-discipline and his battling [against his ego]. These two may be light or hard; they vary in their fullness according to the person's nature, and vary in power according to the variations in his orientation and determination, and to the degree in which the ominous things which have taken over the heart are established therein. What we have just said does not apply only to presence, but applies more generally to the processes of acquiring all the praiseworthy attributes which are the source of good works. The man who wishes to acquire these needs an effort at the beginning, when they come only with toil and hardship; then the matter evolves until they are accompanied by pleasure and repose.

Having learnt this, you should know that presence with God is the very spirit and purpose of all acts of worship; it is what [Sufis of] authority are concerned with and what gnostics stress. Acts which God's servants perform while in a state of distraction are considered by them more likely to result in punishment and veiling than in contemplation and reward. The way to attain to presence with God in acts of worship is for a man to watch for and dispel whatever may distract him.

There are two kinds of distraction: those which come through the senses, including hearing and vision, which are dispelled through seclusion, and, secondly, those which arise from the whisperings of the ego [*nafs*], which distract the heart with various insinuations and passing thoughts, which are dispelled by ignoring them and keeping the heart occupied, either by echoing in the heart the same word that the mouth is uttering, whether it be Qur'ān or invocation, or by listening to and hearing what proceeds from the mouth. The important thing in such situations is to control and guard the heart against everything that reaches it, whether from the *nafs* or the senses. When the servant achieves mastery in this degree of forcible presence he should move on to the degree which lies above it, namely, that of perceiving and holding in his heart the meaning of what is proceeding from his mouth, for instance, *lā ilāha illa'Llāh*, or *Allāhu akbar*. If Qur'ān is being recited, the meaning of what is being recited should be present in the heart. And above this noble degree of presence there is a rank nobler still, which is attained when the heart, while occupied with recitation, invocation or worship, perceives, and is present in the Presence of He Who is Speaker, Invoked and Worshipped. This is indicated by the saying of the Prophet, upon whom be blessings and peace: 'Excellence [*iḥsān*] is to worship God as though you saw Him.' Those who wish to attain this formidable degree of contemplation must thoroughly complete the steps which precede it, as we said before, and fully affirm that the Real God transcends all contingencies; for a man lacking in insight may compromise this transcendence with false imaginings, the like of which the Real far transcends. At this degree, which is to contemplate the Speaker in His words, and the Remembered in His remembrance, there is absence, absorption, and extinction, and other such states as are found among God's people.

Whoever wishes to arrive, let him travel the path, embrace patience and resolution, and roll up his sleeves to devote all his effort and ability to his quest; and let him heed the words of the 'Master of the Faction', al-Junayd, may God's mercy be upon him, who, when asked how he had acquired so many sciences which none of his shaykhs had possessed, pointed to a stair in his house, saying: 'By sitting under that stair with God for thirty years.' It was the custom of al-Shiblī, may God's mercy be upon him, at the outset of his spiritual career, to take a bundle of wooden twigs and seclude himself in an underground dwelling, where, whenever distraction overtook him he would take one and strike himself with it. By the end of the night he would have struck himself enough times to use up the whole bundle.

The beginning of the unveilings [*mukāshafa*] and contemplation [*mushāhada*] that they were able to attain was the effort they made and the hardship they endured, for although these things may be attained without such effort and hardship, this is in fact extremely rare. The man who reaches the degree of presence and intimacy with God then has actually to force himself to attend to the created world or to become involved in any worldly matter when this is necessary for him. At this, his state will have been turned around, from one of forcing himself to be present with God, to one of forcing himself to attend to the world.

One of the greatest supports to the achievement of presence with God is for the servant to make his heart feel that God sees him, his heart, and his inner intention and orientation, rather than his body and the outward form of his actions alone.

Gnostics teach that one of the factors that disturb one's presence with God during the ritual prayer or remembrance [*dhikr*] is for one's heart to be occupied with things other than the Hereafter. They hold that the important thing is to concentrate all one's outward and inner aspect on whatever activity one is engaging in for the sake of God the Exalted, for it will never be accomplished correctly and masterfully unless this be done. Distraction of the heart may even damage the outward form of the act, and not just its inner meaning, as we sometimes see. When presence is not forcibly striven for, acts of worship performed in a state of distraction do not lead one on to a state of presence, although they are not [entirely] lacking in blessings. A man once said to Abū Ḥafṣ:[35] 'I invoke God, but achieve no presence', to which the reply was: 'You should thank God for adorning one part of you with His remembrance.'

THE THIRD RESPONSE

Some further explications

You have also enquired about what praise means, and what it means to attribute transcendence to God. You also ask how one should express one's denial of one's own power and ability [*ḥawl wa-quwwa*], about the meaning of remorse, and asking for forgiveness, and whether these are exclusive to sinners, or general enough to include the ascent from one noble spiritual station to a higher one.

(a) *Tasbīḥ* and *Ḥamd*

You should know that to attribute Transcendence is to attribute holiness as well as exaltation. Its meaning is for the heart to be convinced that in His Essence, Attributes and Acts, the Real (Majestic and High is He!) transcends all resemblance to created beings. He is Holy, Transcendent, and High above partners, likenesses, contingencies which begin and end, aims and causes, and limits of time and location. He transcends any form that may arise in one's mind or imagination, and is beyond being apprehended by thought; for what He is lies beyond the scope of intelligence and the reach of knowledge.

Exaltation [*tasbīḥ*] is often mentioned in the Qur'ān when the Real affirms His freedom from everything that deviators [*mulḥidūn*] attribute to Him that is unworthy of His impregnable perfection. Examples of this include His saying: *O people of the Book! Go not beyond the bounds in your religion, and say not anything but the truth concerning God,* up to *God is but one God; Transcendent is He, above having a son.* [4:171] *They have taken their rabbis and monks as lords* up to *Transcendent is God above what they empartner.* [9:31] *Is it not of their own calumny that they say: God has begotten? They are truly liars* up to *Transcendent is God above what they describe.* [37:151–9]

As for 'praise' [*thanā'*], this is to laud and extol, in other words, to make mention of the qualities of perfection that befit the Praised One, His attributes of loftiness, nobility and majesty, and the gifts and attainments that flow from Him to those who praise Him as well as to others, and His protection of them against various kinds of hardships and opposition. All of these things are to be accompanied by reverence and awe.

One of the acts of worship that most completely contains the various aspects of praise is to utter the phrase *al-Ḥamdu li'Llāh* ['praise is for God!']. Know that God the Exalted is the [only] one who is absolutely transcendent and worthy of praise, in every way and in all senses. This is uniquely and exclusively His, since He is free from all imperfections, and to Him belongs the whole of perfection, because He is the Source of all good; and every attainment, transcendence and praise is real only in His case, and [merely] figurative for others. In effect, neither transcendence nor praise can ever be truly attributed to another, literally or metaphorically; for any creature who either achieves a kind of transcendence or does something which is deserving of praise, never does so by his own power and ability, but only by God's power, will, grace, and mercy; which come from God and belong to Him. The attributing by some people of transcendence by praising or extolling a created being who is indeed free of that which they say he is free of, is but the [manifestation of the] imperfection that belongs to this being's kind. And when they praise him for a quality of perfection that is actually his, they are but attributing transcendence and praise to God. This is known to some people, and quite unknown to others.

Know, also, that God the Exalted stands in no need of

anyone's attribution of transcendence or praise to Him. Those who do so neither free Him from imperfections—for He has none, and it is inconceivable that he have any—nor establish His perfection by their praise—for perfection was ever His, and eternally remains so. The man who attributes transcendence to his Lord, and praises Him, is only attracting benefits and good to himself; and God, in His grace, has promised this to him. The Prophet has said, may blessings and peace be upon him: '*Al-ḥamdu li'Llāh* fills the Scales, and *Subḥān Allāh wa'l-ḥamdu li'Llāh* fills the distance which is between heaven and earth.' And he said: 'God is pleased with a servant who, when he eats a morsel of food, praises and thanks Him for it, and when he drinks a drink, praises and thanks Him for it.' The material bequeathed to us concerning *Subḥān Allāh* and *al-Ḥamdu li'Llāh* is both too voluminous and too well-known to be repeated here.

Those who strive, do so for themselves; for God is surely Independant of the worlds. [29:6]

(b) Ascribing power and ability

You should know that the most comprehensive and inclusive formula for expressing the repudiation of one's own claim to power and ability is *Lā ḥawla wa-lā quwwata illā bi'Llāh* ('there is neither power nor ability save by God'). The Proof of Islam, may God be pleased with him, said: '"Power" [*ḥawl*] is motion, and "ability" [*quwwa*] is aptitude"'. No creature possesses either ability or power over anything save through God, Who is Able and Capable. It is incumbent upon believers to have faith that in whatever God permits them to do or abstain from—as, for instance, in conforming to an injunction, whether by acting or abstaining, or in seeking their provision by resorting to action in the form of crafts and professions, and so on—it is God the Exalted Who creates and originates their intentions, abilities and movements; and that the acts they choose to perform will be attributed to them in the manner known as 'acquisition' [*kasb*] and 'working', and shall be, in consequence, liable to reward and punishment; but that they exercise volition only when God Himself does so, and can neither do nor abstain from anything unless He renders them able to. They possess *not a single atom's weight of the heaven or the earth*, nor do they attain to any partnership in its governance, or become supports to Him.

It is on the ability and power to make choices, which God has granted to His servants, that commands and prohibitions are based. Things which are done intentionally and by choice are attributed to them, and they are rewarded or punished accordingly.

Hence the meaning of *lā ḥawla wa-lā quwwata illā bi'Llāh* is the denial of one's possession of autonomous power and ability, and the simultaneous confession of the existence of that [relative] power and ability to make choices that He has given His servants to be their own.

He who claims that man has no choice or ability, that the acts he selects are identical with the acts he is compelled to do, and that he is in all circumstances coerced is a deterministic [*jabrī*][36] innovator whose false claim would deny that there was any purpose in sending Messengers and revealing Scriptures. By contrast, he who claims that man possesses the will and power to do whatever he does by choice is a Muʿtazilī[37] innovator. But he who believes that a responsible [*mukallaf*] man possesses power and choice to allow him to comply with God's commands and prohibitions, but is neither independant thereby nor the creator of his own acts, has found the *Sunna*, joined the majoritarian community, and become safe from reprehensible innovation. There is a lengthy explanation to this, which follows a rugged road where many have slipped and gone astray; and beyond it is the secret of Destiny, which has always perplexed intelligent minds, and into which the Master of Messengers has commanded us not to delve. So let the intelligent be content with hints, and let it suffice them to believe that everything was created by God, and nothing exists without His will and power. Then let them require their selves to conform to the commandments and prohibitions, and take their Lord's side against their selves in every circumstance. A *ḥadīth* says that '*Lā ḥawla wa-lā quwwata illā bi'Llāh* is one of the treasures of the Garden'. Understand the indication contained in terming it a 'treasure' and you will know that its meaning is among the mysteries; for reward is of the same species as the act. The Prophet has also said, may blessings and peace be upon him: 'Two *rakʿas* in the depths of the night are one of the treasures of goodness.' Their reward comprises a hidden treasure because the time of their occurrence, namely the night, implies this.

It is also reported that '*Lā ḥawla wa-lā quwwata illā bi'Llāh* is a remedy for ninety-nine ailments, the least of which is sorrow.' It is a remedy for sorrow because grief mostly occurs when one misses something one loves, or when a distressful thing occurs; and whenever either of these things occurs people perceive their helplessness and inability to achieve their desired aims; hence they feel sorrow. If at such times they repeat in their heart and with their tongues words which mean that they disavow the possession of any ability or power of their own, then this gives them certitude in their knowledge that they are helpless and weak except where God gives them power and ability, with the result that their sorrow is banished, and their knowledge of their Lord is increased. This can be clearly understood from the Prophet's saying, may blessings and peace be upon him: 'When one believes in destiny, one's sorrow departs.' And in attributing ability and power to His Name, *Allāh*, which is the axis of the Names and the most supreme of them, and in following it on most occasions with the two noble Names which indicate two of the attributes of the Holy Essence, namely, those of Exaltation and Magnitude,[38] lies a sign that He totally transcends and is absolutely holier than the illusions of those who have strayed from the path, are blind to the evidence, and have delved without insight into the secret of destiny and the acts of God's creatures. So take heed!

(c) Remorse, and seeking forgiveness

Remorse [*nadam*] is the turning of the heart, in sorrow and regret, away from something which the servant has committed, and which angers God the Exalted, such as sins or the neglect of obligatory acts. It may also occur following an excessive involvement in permissible pleasures or the neglect of supererogatory devotions. A sincere remorse is one which leads to persevering in earnest, and avoiding neglectfulness. When sound, it includes nearly all the conditions of repentance [*tawba*], which is why the Prophet has said, may blessings and peace be upon him: 'Remorse *is* repentance.' Those who are remorseful about their misbehaviour, but still persist in it, are only jesting, and their remorse will not avail them.

Seeking forgiveness [*istighfār*] means asking God to forgive, which in turn means His concealing the misdeed [from the eyes of others]. When God, by His grace, forgives a sin, he neither exposes its doer to shame, nor punishes him for it, whether in this world or in the next. The highest kind of forgiveness is for God to place a veil, a barrier, between the servant and sins, until it is as though he were free of them. In the context of Prophethood this veil is termed 'inerrancy' [*ʿiṣma*]; and in that of sainthood, 'protection' [*ḥifẓ*]. This is the meaning of God's saying, addressed to the Master of the Inerrant, may the best of blessings and peace be upon him: *Ask forgiveness of your sin, and for believing men and women.* [47:19] And: *That God may forgive you your former and subsequent sin.* [48:2] It is well known that the Prophet was not liable to sin. But He here reminds him of His favouring him with His protection from everything that would distance him from Him, and commands him to pray to Him in that manner; prayer in this context being the consequence of thankfulness, and thankfulness being the cause of further increase. *If you are thankful, I shall give you more.* [14:7] And God knows best.

(d) A distinction between subtle gradations of sins

Know that although obedience is the path to God and the means of approach to His Holy Presence, it may induce in those who are liable to distraction many things which are reckoned among the major sins, such as ostentation, self-admiration, arrogance, the feeling that one has obliged God, forgetfulness of His grace in granting [acts of obedience], and so forth. These may result in the deprivation of the obedient man's reward, and may even lead to painful punishment. The believer who is intent on following the path of seriousness and is concerned to attain salvation should always accuse his own soul [*nafs*], and refuse to give it the benefit of the doubt; he will ask forgiveness even for his acts of obedience, even if no contravention has outwardly occurred, fearful that his soul may have led him into one of these hazardous faults. You now know why one should seek forgiveness even for acts of obedience.

Something even more subtle than this may befall the people of gnosis under some circumstances: they may notice that they have come to find comfort in their virtuous acts [rather than in God], or to rely on them [rather than on God]; and they then turn back to Him in repentance, asking for forgiveness. The same things may again befall them while they pass through the noble stations and states with which they are invested; and they have then to repent and ask forgiveness for them.

For the people of God who divest themselves of all attachment to the worlds, sin is to attend to other than God, whatever this 'other' may be. We see them fleeing fearfully to

God and seeking refuge in Him from states which, if experienced by others, would have been considered great acts of devotion, such as, for instance, setting one's hopes in one's acts of obedience and having thoughts of fear [of God] or of renunciation. It is in this context that you should understand the saying: 'The good deeds of the righteous are the evil deeds of those who are brought nigh to God.'[39] Were it not that the Path is fading away and the lights of realization are setting, we would have said some astonishing things on this subject. *So take heed, O people of intelligence!*

Shaykh Shihāb al-Dīn al-Suhrawardī,[40] may God have mercy upon him, has said:

> There are certain factors which impair spiritual stations, for these latter may be infiltrated by extraneous elements, and the gnostic may fail to perceive this while still in them, and only become aware of this upon rising from one station to a higher one, at which, experiencing an imperfection, he looks back at the former with better insight, and returns to it in order to repair the defect and render it sound. This can only be done through repentance and asking for forgiveness.

This is a summary of what the gnostics have taught, with some explanations and clarifications. Some have interpreted the saying of the Prophet, may blessings and peace be upon him: 'My heart becomes covered, so that I ask God for forgiveness seventy times a day,' along the lines suggested by Suhrawardī, but in fact it is far from bearing any relation whatever to the Muḥammadan rank which embraces all perfection of form and character. I have another interpretation for it, which I can only divulge verbally to those worthy to receive it.

And God knows best.

THE FOURTH RESPONSE

On whom we perceive ourselves as receiving from

You inquire about how one should judge, according to religious criteria, a man of the Path who says: 'Those who receive from the hands of other creatures must be receiving from God, and this by unveiling and tasting, not by faith and knowledge.'

These are the words of a gnostic speaking of his own state and expressing what he beholds. It is the state of someone who is extinct to everything that is other-than-God, absorbed in the contemplation of His majesty and beauty, conscious of no creature, neither feeling nor perceiving anything that exists, deprived of the ability to dispose and choose, no longer perceiving the traces,[41] his secret immersed in the depths of the ocean of secrets, the dark night that is existence effaced by the dawning of the day that is the Object of his contemplation. You behold him behaving with his Lord as the dead body behaves towards its washer, moving only when He moves him. He has lost awareness of all causes by beholding the Causer of all causes, and is extinct to other-than-Him through beholding the act of the One Who chooses and acts. As a noble gnostic once remarked:

> Great is that bewildered youth, perplexed,
> Whose Lord has extinguished his name, and raised him up.
> Time passes, and he knows not its reckoning,
> as he is made to quaff the wine.

A man in this state has been overwhelmed and overmastered by what he is contemplating. He is unable to avoid whatever *wārid*[42] comes to him in this state, while God guards and protects him in whatever proceeds from him while in that condition. Those who are true in these situations never indulge in anything which is contrary to the attributes of servitude [*ʿubūdīya*], even though they stand under no legal responsibility, since they have lost those powers of discrimination upon which [legal responsibility] depends.

The people of realization, may God be pleased with them, are extremely eager to receive and hold this *wārid*, because in it they depart from the physical forms [*rusūm*: of dense existence]; and their human attributes, which are the veil which lies between them and the contemplation of the divine secrets, are effaced.

Know that this state, even should it come, does not persist. If it does, strange things will become manifest in the servant, and he may finally reach to the condition of fading and vanishing. This is a divine favour bestowed by God upon whom He will, and is not to be attained by hopes and the illusions of the *nafs*. Nonetheless, a man can render himself receptive to it by means of proper self-discipline and sincere striving, in conformity to the Book and the Sunna.

A man who merely pretends to be in this condition and to possess the attributes proper to those who have attained it, is deluded, and will be held to account, for because of it he will have left unfulfilled some of the rights which both God and creation have upon him. For it is one of the attributes of the man in Extinction that he cannot be conceived of as loving, fearing or expecting anything from any created being. He will neither thank nor reward any being for a service rendered, for he sees none but God.

Know that the man of Extinction sees God and does not see creation, while the man of Subsistence [*baqā'*]—and there is no Subsistence before the occurrence of true Extinction—sees things by God, and therefore gives each his due, puts each thing in its appropriate place, and fulfils to perfection the rights of the Real as well as those of creation; and this neither distracts him from his Lord nor veils him from his station. The man of Extinction may be subject to flashes of Subsistence, and the man of Subsistence to flashes of Extinction; while the actual spiritual state of a man is that which he experiences most of the time. You hear of men who have reached the state of Subsistence, and yet about whom things are related that bear witness to absorption and Extinction; for instance, that which we hear about Shaykh Abu'l-Ḥasan al-Shādhilī,[43] may God be pleased with him, when he said: 'We love none but God!' Someone said: 'Your ancestor, may blessings and peace be upon him, said: "Hearts are given an intrinsic nature to love those who are good to them," to which the Shaykh replied: "We see no doer of good apart from God; if we must, then as a cloud of dust which you take for something until you examine it more closely, and find it to be nothing at all."' By this he meant that such was the manner in which he saw creation. To express the experience of those who see only God, in both the act of giving and that of withholding, is difficult; language can hardly stretch that far. However, one can recognise the possessor of such a station by its outwardly manifest signs.

The important and indispensable thing, when receiving anything from the hand of a created being, is to do so with both knowledge and courtesy [*adab*], both inward and outward. Outward knowledge implies that you must accept only that which is acceptable in the *Sharīʿa*, while inward knowledge implies that you take nothing, when possessing enough, except with the intention of giving it away; and accept nothing that your ego expectantly desires. The meaning of 'expectant desire' here is hoping and hankering after something from a particular source. Suppressing this is part of inner courtesy, to conform to which is a virtue. The obligation connected to inward knowledge is to know with certainty that the real giver is God the Exalted, for He is the One Who gave to the one who gave to you, commanded him to give, and will reward him with what is nobler and finer than what he gave. He is the One Who cast in his heart the irresistable urges which he could not countermand, made the act of giving pleasant to him, made [the thought of] you occur to his mind, and inspired him with the thought that there was goodness and benefit in doing you a favour; while [in reality] he did a favour only to himself. Now, tell me, can one perceive created beings, or abide with them, as long as one has this particular knowledge of God? Nonetheless, never fail to thank those who render you a service; be kind to them and pray for them, for He has commanded us to do so. He only made them the instruments of benevolent acts, locations for goodness, mediators between Him and His servants, because it pleased Him that this be theirs, and it pleases Him that they be treated accordingly. When you thank them, you are in reality thanking God.

Now we have said this, you have come to know the rules which govern those who take from the hands of created beings, whether they be people of Wayfaring, Extinction, or Subsistence. Take these rules firmly, and act accordingly!

The author of the book *Nourishment for Hearts*,[24] may God show him His mercy, and bring benefit by him, said: 'If you find, to receive a favour of yours, a man of certainty who sees nothing but God, seize the opportunity to do him a favour! Even if his state forces him neither to thank you nor to pray for you, since he does not even see you, his certainty will be more profitable, and weigh more in your balance, than the prayers and thanks of someone else.'

THE FIFTH RESPONSE

(a) Reciting Sūra al-Wāqiʿa **('The Event')**

As for your question about the regular recitation of *Sūra al-Wāqiʿa*, know that the following account has been narrated in this regard: 'To read it each night is to be free from want,' that is, to be independant of other creatures (the kind of 'dependance' meant here being that which shames a man, both in his worldly affairs and in his manly virtue). When Ibn Masʿūd, may God be pleased with him, was told on his deathbed that he had left his children in poverty, he replied: 'I gave each of them a treasure: *Sūra al-Wāqiʿa*.' The special attributes of certain *sūras* and verses of the Qur'ān, and those of the invocations and prayers of the Prophet are not unknown: the books of *ḥadīth* are full of them. Imām al-Ghazālī wrote an entire book on the subject, entitling it: *Unalloyed Gold: The Properties of the Majestic Book.*[44]

The regular recitation of *al-Wāqiʿa* and other *sūras* of the same type, in order to bring benefit to oneself and ward off worldly harm, does not compromise one's intentions or actions. Nonetheless, the motive should not be entirely lacking in religious purpose: since for a servant deliberately to guard himself against depending on others is the best of intentions. For an intelligent believer will not intend, in wanting independance from others and safety for himself and his family, those things which are associated with physical comfort and pleasure; instead his intention will be to free himself from whatever may damage him religiously, of the things which can be seen in many people who suffer from such afflictions. This is why the great men of God are always keenly occupied with asking Him to safeguard the wellbeing [*ᶜāfiya*] of both their souls and their bodies, being fearful of the manner in which their souls, weak and wavering by nature, respond when faced with things that are repellant to them.

The Messenger, may blessings and peace be upon him, repeatedly sought protection against poverty and sickness. He said: 'Poverty is not far from being disbelief [*kufr*]', because people afflicted with it are liable to feel discontented with God's decree, or angered against Divine providence; or at least assailed by some form of anxiety. Sufyān al-Thawrī,[10] may God show him His mercy, once said: 'I do not fear hardships because of the pain they cause me; but I fear that were I to be afflicted with hardship, I might fall prey to disbelief.' Perfection for the servant lies in his being content with his Lord's choices on his behalf, in sufficing himself with His knowledge, and in being more concerned with His choosing and disposing than with his own.

A certain gnostic once said:

> In the regular recitation of *Sūra al-Wāqiᶜa* there lies a secret which increases one's certainty, engenders peace in the heart, and adds to this a serenity, whether one possesses [one's provision] or not. This is because God opens and closes it with a mention of the Appointed Time, and the ways in which people shall differ on that day. Anyone who reflects on this will be too preoccupied with it to attend to any worldly matter which may occur to him. Here, too, God makes mention of the origin of man's creation, how He makes his beginning *a drop of seed expelled* [75:37], and how the crops and the water upon which their subsistence depends originate. He enjoins them to reflect on this, and makes them all aware that they did not possess the power to create, grow and protect their crops, or bring down the rain; and this inculcates the most profound awareness of the Divine power and the pre-existent will and knowledge of

God. When this awareness is coupled with the knowledge that God has guaranteed His servant's provision and sustenance, the heart is pacified, and one then attends to the worship of the Lord. And God knows best.

(b) A caution

A man may persevere in reciting certain *sūras*, invocations, or prayers, for which promises of immediate benefits have been made, and yet see no result. He should not doubt the soundness of these truthful promises, but should rather blame himself, and attribute to himself a deficiency in certainty and concentration. For a man who recites or invokes is not termed a [real] 'reciter' or 'invoker' according to the religious law unless all the conditions are fulfilled, and the fact is that most people fall short of doing this. The essential thing which will make these practices effective and fruitful is to nurture a certainty in the heart that the matter is as it has been said, and to have neither doubts about it nor the desire to put it to trial. One should be truly concentrated, uniting one's outward to one's inward [faculties] in engaging the matter, with one's heart sincerely thinking well of God, and be utterly and attentively oriented towards Him. Rarely do these things come together in a man who is intent on reaching some objective by means of verses and invocations—whatever this objective may be—without this quest becoming his to control and manage at will. So let a servant whose determination falls short and whose earnestness and zeal are deficient blame only himself. *And God is never unjust to the servants.* [3:182]

SIXTH RESPONSE

On Audition

You ask whether a man should still attend audition[45] when he feels his spirit becoming as though agitated during such sessions, and as a result suffers a certain amount of fatigue. Know, may God instruct you, that audition is a hazardous matter, so much so that my master, the lordly *quṭb*, ʿAbdallāh ibn Abī Bakr al-ʿAydarūs,[46] may God be pleased with him and spread his benefit, has remarked: 'For every man whom God guides with this audition, He leads a thousand others astray.'

It must be made clear that the results of audition will depend on the motive behind it. The motive must therefore be a true one, free from capricious and passional desires, and one should listen only to what is deemed permissible by religious criteria. Audition is most beneficial when one listens to the Qur'ān, *Sunna* or appropriate discourses; however, the effects of listening to poetry, fine voices, and rhythmic melodies are also praiseworthy when related to religion; otherwise they are [simply] permissible [*mubāḥ*], and there is no harm in listening as long as they do not depart from the lawful. Our intention in saying these few summary words is to treat the question briefly; otherwise, the writings of the People[47] (in particular, the *Revival*[23] and the *Gifts*[40]) are full to the brim with long explanations of the rules for audition.

As for the man in the state you describe, if he fears that in attending he may slip into showing ostentation or affectation with others, then it is more appropriate for him not to attend. If he has no such fears, but finds no benefit in audition (such as an increase in the determination and energy he feels for his devotions, his yearning for Contemplation, or any other such thing), then it is again better for him not to attend, for no man should subject himself to unprofitable effort. But if he does benefit, and makes religious gains, then he must weigh these against the effort involved, and choose the better and more profitable course. On the whole, gnostics attach no importance to physical discomfort and pain when set against the benefits and gains of the heart, for the essence of their method is the heart's purification and reform, and directing it towards their Glorious Lord. Know this! Success is from God.

SEVENTH RESPONSE

On some of Imām al-Ghazālī's precepts

(a) Knowing a thing is distinct from knowing that one knows it.

You ask about the saying of the Imām, the Proof of Islam, the pride of rightly-guided leaders, the greatest of scholars, Muḥammad ibn Muḥammad ibn Muḥammad al-Ghazālī (may God sanctify his secret and bestow upon us something of his wide spiritual effulgence!): 'The knowledge of a thing is distinct from the knowledge of the knowledge of that thing.' Know that these words are clear, and we shall offer an example to render them more intelligible. You know, for instance, that it is God Who has created you and everything else: this is the knowledge of the thing. You also know that you know that God has created you; this is knowledge of the knowledge, and is distinct from the former. The separation of each from the other is capable of conceptualization.

Al-Khalīl ibn Aḥmad[48] said: 'Men are of four categories: [i] A man who knows, and knows that he knows: this is a learned man, so follow him; [ii] A man who knows but is not aware that he knows: this is a man asleep, so awaken him; [iii] A man who does not know but knows that he does not know: this is a seeker of guidance, so guide him; [iv] A man who does not know, and is unaware that he does not know: this is an ignorant man, so reject him!'

(b) Knowledge brings to fruition spiritual states, and states bring to fruition spiritual stations.

You also ask whether al-Ghazālī's saying: 'Knowledge brings to fruition a state [*ḥāl*], and the state brings to fruition a station [*maqām*]', is an acknowledged fact, since one may gain a different understanding from the statements of other writers.

Know that the position of the Proof of Islam [al-Ghazālī], may God have mercy upon him, is the one to be relied on in this matter, and those who say otherwise are to be discounted. The meaning of what he said can be clarified by explaining one of the stations of certainty, so that the case of other stations may be analogously appreciated.

Know that renunciation [*zuhd*] is one of the noble stations. It is established on the basis of the knowledge of what is stated in the Book, the Sunna, and by the virtuous men of this nation by way of disparagements of the world, criticisms of those who chase after it, and praises of those who turn away from it and are more intent on the hereafter. Following this, if one is given to succeed, one's heart is affected in such a way as to compel one to renounce the world and desire only the hereafter. Knowledge thus comes first, while its consequence is the state.

There then appear from the bodily organs and limbs acts which indicate the presence of this effect, such as shunning the pursuit of worldly riches or the accumulation of material things, and holding to the good works which bring advantage in the Hereafter. This effect then meets contrary influences, such as the insinuations of the devil and the ego, which encourage him to desire the world. Following this onslaught, his state may then change, waver or weaken; it may at times vanish completely (which is why it is termed a 'state'). But when it becomes firmly established and is reinforced, and its roots are deeply implanted in the heart so that no passional thoughts are capable of affecting or shaking it, it is called a 'station'. Thus you have come to know that knowledge brings to fruition a state, and the state brings to fruition a station.

States and stations have signs and marks to indicate how sound and comprehensive they are; these appear on one's outward form and are called 'works'; which are also the result of knowledge, although they pertain only to the outward aspect, this being the difference between them and states. The author of the *Gifts*[40] says that 'states are the initial stages of stations, and the one who becomes firmly established in one of the stations of certainty will thereby possess the state belonging to the station immediately superior to it.' You should be aware of this fact.

Now, there are two types of state: the first is the one we have just mentioned, while the second comprises the noble gifts such as Intimacy [*uns*],[49] Absence [*ghayba*],[50] Intoxication [*sukr*],[51] and Union [*jamᶜ*],[52] which come to a heart illumined with the lights of self-discipline and spiritual effort. States in this category are not the result of knowledge, but of a penetrating concentration which takes the form of sincere transactions and truthful intentions; these were not meant by the *Imām* in his statement. The states often spoken of by the Sufis are those of the second kind. And God knows best.

(c) It is insufficient, in performing an act of obedience to God, to know that it is one.

You also ask about his saying: 'It is insufficient, in performing an act of obedience to God, to know that it is one; it is also necessary to know the timing, procedure, and conditions.'

The 'timing' is the specific time prescribed for its performance. The 'procedure' is the correct manner of this performance, including the correct sequence. (Ritual ablutions and prayers, for instance, are only valid if performed in the correct sequence.) This is obligatory in those acts of worship where it can be conceived to apply. The status of timing and procedure is self-evident. As regards 'conditions', he probably means whatever the validity (or, alternatively, the perfection) of the act of obedience depends on. For example, the possession of reason is a condition for the validity of faith and Islam, and these in turn are the conditions for the validity of obligatory acts, the avoidance of forbidden things, and the seeking of nearness through supererogatory devotions and sincerity with God. And to purify one's intentions from the vice of ostentation is a condition for attaining to the benefits which all the abovementioned actions will yield in the Hereafter. And God knows best.

(d) On involuntary thoughts [*khawāṭir*].

And you ask about his statement, may God be pleased with him, on involuntary thoughts which come into the mind, and whether one is morally accountable for them.

This matter is clear; however, in order to explain it summarily we may say that a thought, whether good or evil, brings neither reward nor retribution as long as it remains indecisive; but in the presence of decision and resolution, it attracts a reward of the same kind as itself.

You also ask about the relationship between these thoughts and the questions he discusses towards the end of the *Book of Fear and Hope*,[53] where he states that 'the inward attributes of a man who is a mixture [of good and evil], such as arrogance, ostentation, envy and their likes, will appear to him after death in horrifying forms which will torment him. This is the rule for everyone who leaves this world before he has purified his inward aspect from such repugnant traits.' If this is indeed the passage you are referring to, then no problem exists, for thoughts are things which occur to the soul, and then reverberate in the breast until their aim is fulfilled—although they may vanish before this. In the *Book of Fear* the author refers to the ruinous attributes which a man may harbour in himself and persistently maintain. They are a category of major sins of the inward, and expose those who possess them to great retribution, both immediate and deferred. Great is the difference between the [ingrained] attributes of the heart and the thoughts that simply occur to it. If we have answered with our exposition the query you intended, then thanks be to God; if not, then send us the specific passage that you found problematic, so that we may clarify it for you, with God's help.

(e) On the relationship between the tongue, the mind, and the heart.

You ask about the following statement of Imām al-Ghazālī in his *Book of the Secrets of Recitation*:[54] 'The tongue is a counsellor, the mind an interpreter, and it is the heart which is influenced.'

The passage is clear: the function of the tongue is to produce the words which convey concepts; the mind listens to these words, extracts the concepts, and then casts them into the heart, which is then influenced by them. The mind is thus the heart's minister and disposer; and, because it mediates between the tongue and the heart, it is called an 'interpreter' in contexts such as this. This applies to the Companions of the Right Hand [*aṣḥāb al-yamīn*], to whom the concepts come during and after the recitation of Qur'ān. The Ones Brought Nigh [*al-muqarrabūn*], on the other hand, actually receive the ideas *before* the recitation, since the concepts are already established in their hearts and blended with their essential realities, so that they are ever present, whether the tongue is actively reciting or not.

(f) On the difference between jealousy for God, and envy.

You also ask about his saying, concerning a man who uses God's favours to disobey Him: 'To wish for those favours to be taken away from him is not a kind of envy, but a jealousy [*ghīra*] on behalf of God the Exalted.'

Know that what he writes, may God show him His mercy, is correct. However, it is better, instead of wishing for the disobedient man to be deprived, to pray for him instead, that he may find guidance and be granted the good fortune of thanking his Lord and using His favours in ways beloved by Him. An example of the first policy is an episode in which Dhu'l-Nūn,[55] may God show him His mercy, once saw a boat carrying some people on their way to bear false witness against an innocent man, and he invoked God against them so that they drowned. When questioned about it he said, 'Martyrdom [*shahāda*] in the sea is better than false witness [*shahāda al-zūr*].'[56]

An example of the second is provided by a tale of Maʿrūf al-Karkhī,[57] may God have mercy upon him. He was once walking with his companions along the banks of the Tigris, when he saw a group of corrupt people in a boat, occupied with drinking and other kinds of dissipation. His companions said to him: 'Master, invoke God against them!' And he raised up his hands, and said: 'O God, just as You have granted them joy in this world, grant them joy in the next!' When his companions asked him about this, he replied: 'If He is to grant them joy in the next world, He shall surely relent towards them.' And, in effect, it was not long before they came before the shaykh, having made their repentance.

Now, the course taken by Maʿrūf is the more perfect, for it displays the attribute of mercy present in God's people, particularly those for whom the [Divine] Attribute of Beauty is unveiled. But the attitude cited by the Imām is also a noble station, that of jealousy on behalf of God, which is more frequently found among those of the elect whose contemplation is that of the Divine Majesty.

You should also know that rightful jealousy [*ghīra*] is of two kinds. The first is for one to be jealous for his Lord when His forbidden limits are violated and His rights neglected; this is also termed 'anger for God', and lies at the root of 'enjoining good and forbidding evil', and detesting the unjust and invoking God against them, as was done by Noah and Moses, may peace be upon them.[58] The second is a man's jealousy for something that is his and does not bear sharing, such as a wife. One may be excessive in this, and [go so far as to] accuse guiltless people. One may also dislike sharing things which are susceptible of sharing, such as knowledge, devotion, honour, and eminence. One may even detest anyone who acquires a share of such things, and all this has nothing to do with the kind of jealousy that is praiseworthy.

As for the jealousy of God the Exalted, it means that He is jealous towards His servants when they serve another, and disobey and flaunt His commands. He is also jealous regarding His servants who claim to share in attributes which are exclusively His, such as Glory and Might, Exaltation and Impregnability; for such attributes are appropriately ascribed only to God, the Real, the Kind, the Compeller; *there is no deity save Him, the Mighty, the Wise.*

EIGHTH RESPONSE

On dream-visions

You also ask about the statement of the most perfect *sayyid*, Zayn al-ᶜĀbidīn ᶜAlī ibn ᶜAbdallāh al-ᶜAydarūs,[59] may God have mercy on him, concerning dream-visions [*ru'yā*]. Now, you should be aware that dream-visions are a fraction of Prophethood.[60] They have a realm of their own which is intermediate between inner unveiling [*kashf*] and outward wakefulness. They are the first things that attend the Saints, just as they attended the Messenger, may blessings and peace be upon him, at the outset of his prophecy. Yet not everyone has dreams of this nature, and they are rarely genuine in the case of people who are doing evil as well as good. Truthfulness of the tongue, and the avoiding of corrupt imaginations and illusions, are preconditions for the truth and righteousness of dreams. People who mix [good with evil] may receive something in the nature of true dreams, but the devil adds falsehoods to them, so that the true and false are inseparably confused when an interpretation is attempted. The man who is under the devil's mastery in his waking state, a time when he is able to listen and understand, will be even more under his sway when asleep and deprived of his sense-faculties. Dream-visions are unaffected by imperfections in one's physical body, provided that one's inner faculties remain sound. However, when one is overpowered by a severe illness, or dominated by one of the natural humours, especially phlegm or black bile, one's dreams may become confused so that one sees a thing in a way that differs from what it is really indicating. Imām al-Ghazālī, may God have mercy on him, also said that it is rare for a man's dream to be true if he is given to dwelling on impossibilities, or busies himself with saying things which lead to no good, or himself believes and perceives things differently from their reality, and then leads others down the same path. You should know this, and reflect on it as it deserves, for it is a valuable insight.

My success is only from God. On Him do I rely, and to Him is my return.

Here end the responses which I wished to provide for your questions; they are brief, but nonetheless contain explanations and clarifications which should prove more than sufficient for people endowed with understanding, and for those for whom indications render unnecessary the need for a full elaboration. 'The best discourse' [as a proverb says], 'is brief yet informative.'

A long time ago you requested me to furnish you with a brief commentary on the poem by Shaykh Abū Bakr ibn ᶜAbdallāh al-ᶜAydarūs Bā-ᶜAlawī;[61] and I shall use this to provide a conclusion to the present treatise, so that we may profit from the shaykh's auspicious and blessed words. May God grant people to benefit from him, and from all His righteous servants!

AFTERWORD

The following is a commentary on some finely-expressed, richly significant verses, which were composed by our master, the lordly pole, the master of the gnostics, the exemplar of all authoritative scholars, Shaykh Abū Bakr, son of Shaykh ᶜAbdallāh al-ᶜAydarūs Bā-ᶜAlawī, the *sharīf*, the Ḥusaynī, may God sanctify his spirit, give him light in his grave, and bestow upon us something of his blessings and secrets, in both the worlds. Āmīn.

The zephyr of reunion has blown!
  with neither connection nor separation;
By virtue of a hidden rising-place,
  in which knowledge has no scope.
For it is the fruit of certainty,
  and the attainment to the rank of perfection.

Now, the Shaykh, may God be pleased with him, uses the word 'zephyr', which is the most subtle and gentle of winds, to designate the Divine gifts and lordly attractions [*jadhabāt*][62] with which God singles out His saints and pure ones. Such are they who ever keep themselves in His Presence, are passionate in His love, concentrate their will in His obedience, roll up their sleeves to serve Him, conform to the usages of spiritual courtesy in His presence, and shun all the animal pleasures and satanic attributes that may distract or distance them from Him. The Shaykh uses the word 'zephyr' to denote this exalted gift, in order to protect the secrets from profanation from alterities.

He describes it as being too holy to be subject either to 'connection' or 'separation', both being attributes of dense bodies which noble secrets and spirits transcend. Since the

Real (Exalted is He!) is beyond being subject to union, it is to be expected that His gifts to His elect and the people of His Presence will also be so.[63] Understand this!

The 'rising-place' is the means to the ascent, and its being 'hidden' is its being too remote and subtle to be grasped either by the external senses or the invisible mind and thoughts. The kind of knowledge caught by the net of the physical senses, the rational faculty, or [even] inspiration [*ilhām*][64] 'has no scope', that is, to encompass [any of] it. People's share in it is only to accept and believe it, since it is neither their prerogative nor does it lie within their scope; for it is part of the particular attribute of the spirit and the prerogative of the secret, since it is the 'fruit of certainty', as the poet says (may God be pleased with him).

'Certainty' [*yaqīn*] is the establishment and supremacy of faith in the heart, in such a fashion as to render instability and doubt inconceivable. The 'fruit of certainty' is unveiling [*kashf*] and vision [*ʿiyān*]. Unveiling is the state of the man of certainty, while certainty is his station. Certainty, on the other hand, is the state of the believer, while faith is his station. The believer has flashes of certainty, while the man of certainty has flashes of unveiling. The 'attainment to the rank of perfection' denotes unveiling, which is the first step in the stations of contemplation [*mushāhada*], which is perfection.

> Hence: emulation, then guidance,
> then selection—state above state.
> Whoever holds to the acts and the certainty
> that are required of him, shall obtain
> Indwelling in the gardens of His intimacy,
> and shall pick the fruits of arrival.

'Emulation' means following the Messenger, may God's blessings and peace be upon him, in his character, conduct, and words, and taking on his courtesies and customs, both inward and outward. The lights of guidance will cascade upon those who do this well and properly, sincerely for the sake of God the Exalted; for guidance is the result of excellence in emulation and of self-discipline. God the Exalted has said: *Those who strive in Us, We shall guide to Our paths.* [29:69] This guidance is nothing other than the unveiling of the unequivocal Truth and the reception of things from the world of the Unseen. But this, and self-discipline, are preceded by two things, one of which is 'guidance through clear exposition' [*hidāyat al-bayān*], and the other 'guidance through providential success' [*hidāyat al-tawfīq*].[65]

'Selection' is to attain the realities of certainty, and the outpouring of the gifts which result from closeness to He Who is Mighty and Firm. Just as 'Guidance' is a state higher than that of 'Emulation', being its fruit, so also is 'Selection' higher than 'Guidance', being its spirit and purpose. It denotes God's selection of His servant to receive the gnosis and love of Him, the unveiling of the secrets of His Presence, and the contemplation of the lights of His holy Essence and Attributes. Know this!

It is the nature of a sincere man of sound disposition [*mustaqīm al-fiṭra*], when he hears of these noble experiences and contemplations, to yearn for them. The Shaykh therefore gives him good tidings, and informs him of the way which leads to them, by saying: 'Whoever holds to [the acts and the certainty] that are required of him ...'. 'Holding to' means persistence and constancy. Both acts and certainty 'are required of' God's servants: an 'act' here denoting an action in obedience, which has external aspects which pertain to the physical faculties, as in the case of the forms of the ritual Prayer, alms, and so on; and also inner aspects which characterize the outer aspect of the heart: these are the praiseworthy traits of character, such as humility, renunciation, contentment, and so forth. The inner aspect of the heart, in turn, is the locus of 'certainty', which, as we have said, means 'true, sincere faith'. God, in His grace, has made it possible for a servant to attain to certainty, for He has set up the way of perseverance in acts of worship, reflection on the kingdom of the earth and the heavens, and meditating on the revealed signs [which are the verses of the Qur'ān]. When a man's certainty becomes strong, and both his inward and outward aspects are made beautiful by the continuous performance of good works, he attains to his Lord's nearness, is given to dwell in the delightful 'Gardens of Intimacy', and 'picks the fruits of arrival' to His noble Presence. These 'fruits' are the openings [*mufātaḥāt*], intimate comforts [*mu'ānasāt*], lordly communings and conversations, and other experiences known to the people of God. *That is God's favour; which He bestows upon whom He will of His servants.* [57:21]

These are realized sciences,
  whose exponents are excellent men indeed.
No doubt is there in their certainty,
  nor waywardness in their guidance.
They emulated, then struggled,
  then contemplated, and the impossible vanished.

Having mentioned the subtle unveilings and contemplated realities that the Real conferred upon him, and following this with an exposition of the path that leads to them—as an invitation to God the Exalted, and a counsel to His servants—the Shaykh, may God grant benefit by him, now begins to explain the nature of these 'openings' and that 'path'. He says: 'These are realized sciences,' referring to the sciences obtained by those who, being qualified, see with the light of God, having passed from the narrow straits of imitation [*taqlīd*] to the open expanse of unveiling, and having refused to content themselves with information rather than vision—in contrast to those whose minds are inflexible, who stand by the opinions they have formed and by the intelligence and perspicacity they think they possess. Such people sometimes deny the sciences of the Sufis, because these sciences are beyond their reach and capacity to acquire. In the belief that no kind of knowledge can be beyond their grasp, they deny that of which they are ignorant. Because it is difficult for such minds to accept the inner knowledge of the Sufis, let alone attain to it, al-Junayd, may God show him His mercy, once said: 'To believe in this science of ours is itself [akin to] sainthood.'

The Shaykh next praises those people of God who do attain this knowledge, by saying: 'whose exponents are excellent men indeed.' An 'excellent' man is he who has mastered his soul, cleansed and purified it from vices, adorned it with the virtues, severed all bonds attaching his heart to the worlds, turned inwardly as well as outwardly towards the Divine Presence, established his heart in the attitudes of unification and singlehearted concentration, and his outer form in that of service to God the Exalted, as is the attribute of servants.

The Sufis are the people who fit the above description, whose certainty is never tarnished with wavering or any doubt, and whose guidance, which comprises their sciences and their works, is never mingled with error, deviation from the truth, or inclination to falsehood. They are never satisfied with less than this as concerns their faith and certainty, and therefore impose forms of discipline and struggle upon their souls, until the oceans of their souls become pure and limpid, and they actually attain to the unseen knowledges which the revealed Law had obliged them to believe in. Thus do their sciences and their works stand remote from ignorance, secure from misguidance; for they have taken them from their source, and dug them from their mine.

This condition, however, they only achieve once they have acquired the good manners prescribed by the Law, and have learnt the necessary sciences of faith [*īmān*] and Islam, then energetically practiced what they had learnt, struggling against their egos and refining their characters by means of various disciplines and austerities. It is to this that the Shaykh refers when he says, 'They emulated'; the term 'emulation' denoting, in this context, the acquisition and practice of necessary knowledge. 'Then struggled', in turn, refers to the disciplining [*riyāḍa*] and refining [*tahdhīb*] of the soul. Once they have these two foundations fully secured (knowledge and the practice of it on the one hand, and effective discipline of their souls by weaning them from their habitual and familiar activities, together with sincere concentration on God the Exalted, on the other), their inner aspects become illuminated, their inward eyes open, and they thus contemplate the world of the *Malakūt*,[66] and experience the essential realities of the *Lāhūt*.[67] 'The impossible then vanishes': in other words, disappears from perception (as for its real existence, it was ever-vanishing). The 'impossible' here denotes that which has no independant reality of its own, and no autonomous existence when considered in itself; and this is the inevitable attribute of all that is not God the Exalted.

The Shaykh, may God be pleased with him, then says:

They had the 'knowledge of certainty', then its 'eye',
  nay rather, its 'truth'; no conjectures remain.
They were extinguished to the universe entirely,
  when the rising-star of Majesty appeared.
It revived them after they had been dead,
  through union at the witnessing-place of Beauty.

Know that the term 'Knowledge of Certainty' [*ʿilm al-yaqīn*] refers to sincere faith supported by sound proof and clear evidence. The 'Eye of Certainty' [*ʿayn al-yaqīn*] is one degree higher: it is for a man to lose the need for evidence, since the truth appears to him either as actual vision, or nearly so. The 'Truth of Certainty' [*ḥaqq al-yaqīn*] is the highest degree, being known as the unconditioned and supreme unveiling, and belongs exclusively to the greatest among saints, the elect among the chosen gnostics. It is in this degree that the prophets and their perfected heirs, the True People of God [*ṣiddīqūn*], are firmly established.

As for his saying, may God grant benefit by him: 'No conjectures remain', this signifies that no scope for doubt or uncertainty can any longer exist.

Complete 'extinction' [*fanā'*][68] from the cosmos is a noble state attained by the People of God. It has many sublime and subtle meanings, of which the one intended here is the extinction of the person's perception of himself and all other created things. This extinction occurs at the appearance of the Real's Attributes of Majesty and Compulsion.[69] As these become unveiled, formal human traces are extinguished, and all vestiges of the cosmos vanish. When such an extinction occurs, the Living Sustainer manifests Himself to them in His Attributes of Beauty and Gentleness, whereupon their spirits are given life, their secrets are revived, while their formal traces and habits remain in the state of death induced in the 'extinction by Majesty'. God, Transcendant is He, then keeps them for as long as He wills in this state of 'contemplating the Beauty', which is termed 'Union' [*jam*ᶜ]. Here their spirits find the inexpressible joy of proximity and the delight of the intimacy which lovers grieve for when it is gone, and for which the people of realization yearn. It is to this great joy and bliss that Ibn al-Fāriḍ[70] refers in the following words:

> Each of those nights of my life which passed
> with the loved ones, was a wedding-night!
> After leaving them, nothing was dear to my eye;
> my heart, remembering them, found solace in nought else.
> O paradise from which the soul falls ennobled!
> Did I not yearn for the Lasting Abode, I would perish from grief.

The poems of Ibn al-Fāriḍ, may God spread his benefit, contain many other allusions to the subject we have just discussed, as do the writings of Shaykh al-Sūdī,[71] and other well-grounded gnostics who were qualified to give such indications.

Now, the station into which the Real moves such of them as He wishes to be of benefit to His servants is more perfect and noble than *fanā'*; it is known as the station of Subsistence [*baqā'*].[72] Here the gnostic returns to creation [*al-rujū*ᶜ *ilā al-khalq*], and summons mankind to God. He forces himself to assume their manner of living, so that there may exist some degree of harmony between him and them, which makes it possible for them to respond to his summons. A full exposition of this matter would be very lengthy; and would, moreover, involve subtle concepts and hidden mysteries which are not to be entrusted to the pages of a book, lest they be read by the unqualified, who might then claim these states as their own and thus stray from the Straight Path.

The Shaykh, may God be pleased with him, goes on to declare:

> Until their gold was made so pure,
>   that no wealth could ever equal it.
> The universe has submitted to them,
>   and differs not from their disposing.
> This is real kingship, without dispute,
>   without withdrawal or contravention.

Having explained the state of extinction which takes place during the contemplation of the Majesty and the Beauty, the Shaykh then specifies the results of such a contemplation, including the purification of the soul of its areas of thoughtlessness [*ruʿūnāt*] and its dense attributes. To clarify this: the wayfarer, however thoroughly he may discipline his *nafs* and struggle against it, nevertheless retains certain residues of thoughtlessness and attachments to created things and habits; and these are never entirely erased before the advent of full extinction. This is why no wayfarer is qualified to be a shaykh and a summoner to God before he has reached the states of extinction and subsistence.

There is [the common variety of] gold, in which traces of other substances remain; and there is pure gold. The inner essence of these gnostics becomes purified from the contingencies represented by material bodies, and from all attachments to the worlds. Hence their gnoses, sciences, character traits and works become such that no wealth can possibly equal them—the 'wealth' here referring to the wealth of those who have not attained states equal to theirs. 'Wealth' [*māl*] means whatever is of benefit, and in this context the benefits referred to concern God and the hereafter. When their desires melt into nothingness, their will and wish to make their own choices are extinguished. They have neither desire nor purpose in whatever is not God and does not bring them closer to Him. The created worlds obey such a person, and submit to him, just as he has obeyed and submitted to his Creator; for whoever is God's, God is his, and when God the Exalted is his, the created worlds in all their entirety obey and submit to Him. In one of God's revealed scriptures it is written: 'O son of Adam! I am God, Who says: "Be!" and it is. Obey Me, and I shall make you say to a thing "Be!"' and it is.' Anything that a gnostic wishes for or desires will occur, by God's power, in the same manner that he wishes it. However, since his will, desire, deliberation and choice are extinguished, he only desires and chooses that which God desires and chooses: so that his purpose becomes none other than God's. Understand this, for it is a subtle thing!

By his concern and concentration a gnostic is capable of influencing whatever he directs himself towards. However, he never does this unless he has divine permission. The fact that the created worlds are obedient to God's saints is well-known, having been established through parallel chains of transmission [*tawātur*]. It often happens to wayfarers who are on the verge of the degrees of unveiling but have yet to enter them completely, that [palpable] benefits are yielded through spiritual concentration and orientation; so that these wayfarers are strengthened by the events that are wrought through them. These also happen with the people of Extinction; who, however, are scarcely aware of them, because of their absorption in God and unawareness of all created things. By contrast, such things seldom happen with the people of Subsistence, who are responsible for the task of summoning people to God the Exalted, since they serenely depend on Him, and are content with His judgements and decrees, so that their concern and concentration are rarely focused on any such thing. They may be permitted to demonstrate certain supernatural things, either to strengthen a seeker's flagging resolution, or to challenge an obstinate denier of God's signs or of His special favours upon His saints. However, were a gnostic to concentrate on a mountain so as to make it vanish, or a sea in order to turn it dry, there would be nothing in this but God's power. Furthermore, the gnostics show only disdain for those who desire such *karāmāt*[73] and choose to pursue them for their own sake. They say: 'The [real] *karāma* is *istiqāma* [rectitude]', which denotes excellence in following the Messenger, may God's blessings and peace be upon him, both outwardly and inwardly. No-one attains to such supernatural things until, by discipline, his soul becomes exceedingly subtle, and he gains the ability to guard the secrets and strips himself of all self-oriented desires. And if any such event should ever manifest itself to someone who has not mastered all these things, then it will be a temptation [*fitna*] for him, unless God guard and protect him. God's saints attain to a protection [*taḥarruz*] from enslavement to the created worlds, an invulnerability to material contingencies, utter devotion to Him, and concentration on Him by relinquishing everything, whatever it may be, that may distract and separate them from His Presence. This is 'true kingship', the possessor of which is to be envied, and the establishment and maintenance of which requires neither servants, wealth, arrangements nor preoccupation. It is free of competition with alterities, safe from being disputed by villains, remote from misery, trouble and adversity. It transcends discontinuity, isolation, evanescence, and termination, since these are the changes to which kingship in this world is subject, and which otherworldly kingship transcends. The noblest degree of 'kingship' is for a man to be king of his own soul and passions, dependant on none but God, and willing and desiring nothing of either world but His nearness and good-pleasure. This is the attribute of God's saints and elect (may He be pleased with them, and they with Him). *Those are God's faction; surely, the faction of God shall be triumphant*. [58:22]

In these verses, despite their brevity, the Shaykh, may God be pleased with him and spread his benefit, has included a mention of the openings that God granted him and caused him to attain to, the unveiling and contemplative visions that He conferred upon him, the path that leads to God from beginning to end, a description of God's saints, and of the main privileges they are given pertaining to their nearness to God: the gift of purity from the soiling attachment to the ephemeral worlds, the ability to influence beings at will, and the true kingship that neither subsides nor comes to an end.

> The poem is finished; offer prayers for the Prophet,
> he whose words and acts were refined;
> And his Companions, lords of mankind,
> and his House, best of all houses.

It is thus time for the Shaykh to conclude his verses, having helped the sincere seeker, and favoured the firm aspirant with an explanation of the path to God, so that no further clarifications need be made. He ends by urging his readers to pray blessings on the Messenger of God, may God's blessings and peace be upon him. This 'blessing' is God's mercy, together with a glorification whichs befits the noble rank of Prophethood. By concluding in this wise, with an exhortation to pray blessings on the Prophet, the poet draws attention to, and proclaims, the fact that everything that the Shaykh, or any other gnostic, experienced, was but a consequence of thorough emulation and perfect following of the Messenger, may God's blessings and peace be upon him, 'whose words and acts were refined'. For his speech, may God's blessings and peace be upon him, was the decisive truth, free from everything that people mingle with their words, whether of lies or other imperfections. God the Exalted says: *He speaks not from caprice; it is nought but a revelation revealed.* [53:3] His acts, too, were refined, and free from the imperfections that spoil human actions. Being aided with inerrancy, and chosen for the Divine Revelation, he spoke and acted solely at the Lord's command. Blessed are those that emulate him, are guided by him, and practice his *sunnas*! And alas, alas for those who diverge from following him, are sluggish in responding to his call, and whose conduct departs from his guidance and *sunna*!

'His Companions' denotes those who accompanied him during his lifetime, believed in him, emigrated to him, supported his religion, struggled with him, and transmitted what they heard of his utterances and saw of his acts. Because of these privileges and merits, which are exclusively theirs, they became the 'lords of mankind', and the imāms of right-guidance.

His 'House' denotes his relatives, who combine blood-bonds with ties of religion; and they are the closest and most beloved to him. God has made it incumbent upon the Nation to love and treat them kindly; He has honoured them with purity from defilement.[74] They are the 'best of houses' because they are the house of he who was the best and most honourable of all creation, may blessings and peace be upon him. This honour is not entirely theirs, however, unless they follow their master, he with whom God has honoured them. For of all people, they are the most obliged and deserving to do so. Those of them who neglect to do so, and fail to expend their best efforts to this end, are more deserving of the censure and ill-fortune which befall those who turn away from following the Chosen One; and they will be subjected to a greater share of this than the others. As for those members of the Prophetic House whose emulation is thorough: their honour and merit are greater, more perfect, higher and finer than that of others of similar conduct.

O Lord God! Grant us perfection in following Your Messenger, upon whom be blessings and peace, in his character, conduct and speech. Help and guide us to achieve this; grant us sincerity and truthfulness in doing this, make us live and die in this manner, until the Day You reunite us to Your Prophet, in Your Abode of Honour, remaining pleased with us always, in goodness and wellbeing, O Most Merciful of the merciful!

Here end the words I have been able to record concerning the verses of my master the Shaykh. I do not claim that what I have written conveys his exact intention, but it represents something of what I have understood from his words, and it is of the truth. If it does conform to what the Shaykh intended, then God be praised; if not, then it is still part of what is correct and will benefit, God willing, those of our companions and other beloved ones attached to us who shall read it.

I do confess, from certainty, not from conjecture and guesswork, that I am bereft and devoid of the realities of the people of God, of their experiences and praiseworthy ways. However, I know that in myself I harbour love and attachment to them, an inclination to imitate them and increase their number, together with thinking-well and trusting in them and in all the Openings which God grants them, which are the experiences of unveiling and contemplation. I ask God to join me unto them, and to grant me, by His grace, something of their privileged gifts of gnosis and love. It has been handed down [in *ḥadīth*] that 'A man is with those he loves,' 'He who imitates a people is one of them,' and 'He who increases a people's numbers is one of them.' However, the path of this People has faded, its formal activities have shrivelled and its landmarks are obliterated for the lack of sincere people, so much so that today there is hardly a single sincere seeker of it, while discoursing about it has come to be perceived as nothing more than eloquence and artful expression. *Wa-lā ḥawla wa-lā quwwata illā bi'Llāh*.

How excellent are the words of Shaykh Abū Madyan,[75] may God be pleased with him, in his poem which begins with the words, 'The delight of life is only in the company of the *fuqarā'*,' where, like myself, he also offers an apology and a confession, and announces the effacement of the Way:

> And know that the People's way is effaced:
> you have seen the state of he who claims it today.
> When shall I see them; how can it be mine to see them?
> or when shall the ear hear news of them?
> How could one such as I keep their company,
> at watering-places which know no turbidity?
> I love them, I serve them, I put them before myself,

with my life, and especially a group among them:
Men of noble traits, who, wherever they have sat,
leave that place wreathed in fragrance unending.
Sufism guides their characters to subtlety,
the fine concord between them delights my eye.
They are my folk, my love, my loved ones, who
are worthy to walk in robes of pride and glory.
May my gathering to them in God, wherever done,
yield remission of my sins, and His forgiveness.

Here ends the book entitled *Gifts for the Seeker, being some Answered Questions*. May God render it purely for His sake, and make of it a means to His mercy and good-pleasure. May He forgive us everything it contains that diverges from the truth and inclines towards falsehood, or is the fruit of caprice, or is blemished with ostentation or affectation. May He also forgive the one who provided the motive for writing it, the one who wrote it, those who read or hear it, our parents and loved ones, and all other Muslims. And praise is for God.

O Lord God! We know and are certain that whatever good thing we possess, inner or outward, religious or worldly, is from You and no-one else. You have no partner! May You be praised and thanked! We seek the protection of Your noble Countenance against the loss of blessings and the onset of misfortune. We seek, by Your grace, that You treat us in accordance with Your goodness and generosity, for though we be unworthy of that, You are not! Lord, forgive, and have mercy, for You are the Most Merciful! *And peace be upon the Messengers; and praise is for God, Lord of the Worlds.*

Its dictation was completed early on Friday the fifteenth of Muḥarram, the first month of the year 1072[76] of the Prophet's Emigration, may the best of blessings and peace be upon him.

Lord God, bless our master Muḥammad,
his House and Companions, and
grant them abundant peace,
until the Day of Reckoning.
And praise is for God,
Lord of the Worlds.

TRANSLATOR'S NOTES

1 Saʿīd ibn ʿĪsā al-ʿAmūdī (d. AH 671/CE 1273). The first and greatest of the Sufis produced by the house of al-ʿAmūdī, the Ḥaḍramawt branch of the Ṣiddīqīs (the descendants of Abū Bakr al-Ṣiddīq). He received his investiture into Sufism at the hands of al-Ghawth Abū Madyan, became a disciple of al-Faqīh al-Muqaddam, and called people to the Real until his death at the age of 96.

2 ʿAlī ibn Abī Ṭālib (d.40/661). The Prophet's cousin and son-in-law, he succeeded ʿUthmān ibn ʿAffān to the Caliphate, thus becoming the fourth and last of the 'Rightly-guided Successors.' He died in Kufa at the age of 63, at the hands of an assassin from the Khārijī sect.

3 ʿAbdallāh ibn Masʿūd (d.32/653). One of the earliest men to accept Islam in Mecca. He received the Qur'ān directly from the Blessed Prophet, was one of the most learned Companions, and one of the seven most prolific in giving legal opinions, the other six being Ibn ʿAbbās, ʿUmar, Ibn ʿUmar, ʿĀ'isha, Zayd ibn Thābit, and ʿAlī ibn Abī Ṭālib.

4 ʿAbdallāh ibn ʿAbbās (d.68/687). Cousin to the Blessed Prophet, being the son of his uncle al-ʿAbbās. Called the 'Interpreter of the Qur'ān' by the Prophet and 'Scholar of the *Umma*' by succeeding generations, he was the most prolific of the Companions in giving *fatwās*, or legal judgements, and was one of the seven who narrated more than a thousand *ḥadīths*, the others being Abū Hurayra, Ibn ʿUmar, Anas ibn Mālik, ʿĀ'isha, Jābir ibn ʿAbdallāh, and Abū Saʿīd al-Khudrī.

5 ʿAbdallāh ibn ʿUmar (d. 74/693). The son of the second Caliph, ʿUmar ibn al-Khaṭṭāb. As can be seen from the previous two notes, he was a leading scholar; but he was also celebrated for his piety, generosity, and meticulous care in following even the smallest details of the *Sunna*.

6 Abū Hurayra (d.57/677). The best-known of the People of the Bench (*ahl al-ṣuffa*): a group of the poorest Companions who slept in an area of the Mosque next to the rooms of the Blessed Prophet. He is also remembered as the most prolific of all *ḥadīth* narrators.

7 ʿUrwa ibn al-Zubayr (d.94/713). One of the 'Seven Scholars of the Hijaz.' He was the son of al-Zubayr ibn al-ʿAwāmm, the illustrous Companion, and Asmā', the daughter of Abū Bakr al-Ṣiddīq. He received from his aunt ʿĀ'isha many of the *ḥadīths* which she had heard from the Blessed Prophet.

8 al-Ḥasan al-Baṣrī (d. 110/728), sometimes called al-Ḥasan ibn Abi'l-Ḥasan. A leading Follower (i.e. a member of the second Muslim generation), a disciple of Imām ᶜAlī ibn Abī Ṭālib, and the main link between Imām ᶜAlī and most of the Sufi chains of transmission.

9 Qatāda (d. 117/735). A 'Follower' of Basra, who was an expert in *ḥadīth* and the Qur'ānic sciences.

10 Sufyān al-Thawrī (d. 161/778) was a Kufan scholar and ascetic of the third generation of Muslims (*tābiᶜī al-tābiᶜīn*). A noted *mujtahid*, he died in hiding from the ruler of the day, afraid that he might be forced to accept the position of chief judge of Kufa.

11 Abū Bakr al-Shiblī (d. 334/846). A Sufi of Baghdad and successor of Imām al-Junayd.

12 ᶜUmar ibn al-Khaṭṭāb (d. 23/644), narrator of the *ḥadīth* given in the next note. The second Rightly-guided Caliph, known as *al-Fārūq*, the Discerner. He was assassinated in Medina by a Zoroastrian while he led the congregation in prayer, and was buried in the chamber of ᶜĀ'isha next to the Blessed Prophet and Abū Bakr.

13 This refers to a *ḥadīth* authenticated by Imām Muslim, and very frequently quoted because it contains the three main dimensions of Islam, namely doctrine, ritual practice, and spirituality. ᶜUmar ibn al-Khaṭṭāb, who narrated the *ḥadīth*, said: 'When we were sitting one day with God's Messenger, may God's blessings and peace be upon him, a man came to us whose clothes were very white, whose hair was very black, who showed no signs of travel, and who was not known to any of us. He sat before the Prophet, may God's blessings and peace be upon him, and, putting his knees against his, and his palms on his thighs, said: 'O Muḥammad! Tell me about Islam!' The Messenger of God, may God's blessings and peace be upon him, replied: 'Islam is to attest that there is no god other than God, and that Muḥammad is the Messenger of God, to establish the Prayer, to give the *Zakāt*, to fast Ramaḍān, and to go on pilgrimage to the House if one is able to do so.' And the man said: 'You have spoken truly,' so that we wondered at him, how he questioned and then confirmed his veracity. Then he said: 'Tell me about *Īmān* (faith)', and the Prophet replied: 'To believe in God, His angels, His Books, His Messengers, the Last Day, and in destiny, whether it be good or evil.' He said: 'You have spoken the truth. And tell me about *iḥsān* (excellence).' He replied: 'It is to worship God as if seeing Him, for if you see Him not, He sees you.' He said: 'Tell me then about the Hour (of Judgement).' And he replied: 'The one who is asked knows no more about it than the questioner.' Then he said: 'Tell me then about its signs', and the Prophet replied: 'For the slave-girl to give birth to her mistress, and to see barefoot, naked, destitude shepherds constructing ever-higher buildings.' Then he departed, and, a while

later, the Prophet said: 'O ᶜUmar, do you know who the questioner was?' 'God and His Messenger know best,' I replied, and he told me: 'That was Gabriel, who came to instruct you in your religion.'

14 Ḥudhayfa ibn al-Yamān (d.36/656) was unique in that while the other Companions were constantly asking the Blessed Prophet about virtue and goodness, he asked about evil and temptations, saying: 'I questioned God's Messenger, may God's blessings and peace be upon him, about evil, fearful that it might overtake me.' He thus received from the Blessed Prophet a detailed knowledge of the discords and seditions which were to occur among members of the Nation, as well as the ability to recognise hypocrites for what they were, despite their outward conformity to the tenets of Islam.

15 ᶜUmar used to invite Ibn ᶜAbbās to sit among the elders, and it seems that some of them disliked the introduction of a man so young into their circle. In order to demonstrate Ibn ᶜAbbās's superiority he asked them: 'What do you have to say about God's saying, *When God's victory comes, and the conquest?*' Although they all knew that the 'conquest' in question referred to that of Mecca, some remained silent while others replied: 'We are instructed to praise and thank God, and seek His forgiveness whenever we are granted victory and conquest.' At this, ᶜUmar asked Ibn ᶜAbbās for his opinion, and was told that this was God's sign to the Prophet that *God's victory*, and *the conquest*, would foretoken the end of his life. This interpretation, which none of the older scholars present were aware of, was confirmed by ᶜUmar as being conformable with his own knowledge on the subject.

16 'I am the city of knowledge', said the Blessed Prophet, 'and ᶜAlī is its gate. Whoever seeks that knowledge, let him come to the gate.' This *ḥadīth* is to be found in the compilations of al-Ḥākim, al-Ṭabarānī and Ibn ᶜAdī.

17 *Ḥudūd* (the plural of *ḥadd*), are the statutory punishments, fixed sentences for major crimes such as murder, armed robbery, adultery, drunkenness, slander and so forth. Punishments for lesser crimes are generally left to the discretion of the judge, and are known as *taᶜzīr*.

18 Dawūd al-Ṭā'ī (d. about 165/782). A scholarly pupil of Imām Abū Ḥanīfa. He was also a great Sufi, being the teacher of Maᶜrūf al-Karkhī.

19 Abū Ḥanīfa al-Nuᶜmān (d. 150/767) was the founder of the Ḥanafī school of Islamic law, one of the four major schools recognised in Sunni Islam. He was of Persian extraction, and is believed to have been one of the *Tābiᶜī al-Tābiᶜīn*, although some of his disciples have claimed for him the status of a Follower.

20 The Opening of Lordship (*al-fatḥ al-rabbānī*): the unveiling of the

Divine Attributes of Lordship, which are those that manifest God's solicitude for His creation.

21 The 'Faction' (*al-ṭā'ifa*) is a name commonly given to the early Sufis.

22 Abu'l-Qāsim al-Junayd (d.298/910). The 'Master of the Faction'. Most of the Sufi chains of initiation found in the world today are traced back to the Blessed Prophet via this celebrated Sufi of Baghdad. He was also well-known for his legal expertise.

23 *Iḥyā' ʿUlūm al-Dīn:* the *Revival of the Religious Sciences.* The comprehensive master work of Imām al-Ghazālī, which contains a thorough guide to Islamic devotional and spiritual method.

24 *Nourishment for Hearts (Qūt al-Qulūb).* One of the most widely respected texts on Sufism, written by Abū Ṭālib al-Makkī (d.386/996).

25 Imām Abū Ḥāmid al-Ghazālī (d.505/1111), known as the 'Proof of Islam', one of the greatest scholars produced by the Islamic tradition. The author of definitive works on Shāfiʿī jurisprudence, law, theology and logic, he is buried near Mashhad in Central Asia.

26 Al-Ḥātimī is the tribal name of al-Shaykh al-Akbar, Muḥyi'l-dīn ibn ʿArabī (d.638/1240), author of many works on Sufism, the best known of which are *The Meccan Openings* (*al-Futūḥāt al-Makkīya*), and *The Bezels of Wisdom* (*Fuṣūṣ al-Ḥikam*). His tomb, renovated and adorned in 1517 by order of the ulema of the day, is at Damascus.

27 ʿAbd al-Qādir al-Jīlānī (d.561/1166) was a Ḥasanī sayyid, the founder of the Qādirīya order, and a jurist of both the Shāfiʿī and the Ḥanbalī schools of law, which he taught in Baghdad.

28 Between death and resurrection, man remains in a state known as the Intermediate Realm (*barzakh*). See Imām al-Ḥaddād, tr. Badawi, *The Lives of Man* (London: Quilliam Press, 1991), pp.41–51.

29 Ibn ʿAṭā'illāh of Alexandria (d.707/1307). The successor of Shaykh Abu'l-ʿAbbās al-Mursī, who was himself the successor of Shaykh Abu'l-Ḥasan al-Shādhilī. Shaykh Ibn ʿAṭā'illah taught at al-Azhar university, and wrote several books on Sufism, including the work quoted here, *Miftāḥ al-Falāḥ* (printed in Cairo, 1961 CE).

30 *Taḥmīd* is the phrase *al-Ḥamdu li'Llāh,* the formula used for expressing one's gratitude for God's favours.

31 *Tasbīḥ* is the phrase *Subḥān Allāh,* used to affirm God's transcendance.

32 A *wird* is any regularly repeated devotion, whether involving the Qur'ān, prayers, or anything else.

33 *Dhikr*: the practice of recollecting God, often through set formulas which, when recited with presence of mind at particular times, yield a specific spiritual benefit.

34 Abū Bakr al-Ṣiddīq (d.13/634). The first adult man to accept Islam, and the first 'Rightly-guided Caliph'. He was also the father of ʿĀ'isha, and was known for his gentle and sensitive temperament.

35 Abū Ḥafṣ al-Ḥaddād of Nishapur (d.266/879). One of the earliest

Sufis, mentioned in the *Treatise (Risāla)* of al-Qushayrī. His title 'al-Ḥaddād' is to be taken literally, since he was indeed a blacksmith by trade.

36 The Jabrīya were a sect of fatalist heretics who denied the existence of free will.

37 The Muʿtazilites were a sect who diverged from orthodox Sunni Islam over a number of theological issues. They held, for instance, that man creates his own actions independantly of God, that God cannot will people to disobey Him, since this would amount to an imperfection on His part, and that He is constrained to do what is best for His creatures, since were he to do otherwise this would again be an imperfection on His part. The answers to these pseudo-problems are to be found in the doctrinal expositions of Imām al-Ashʿarī and his followers. See ʿAbd al-Ḥaqq Muḥaddith Dihlawī, *Perfection of Faith*, tr. Yusuf De Lorenzo (Islamabad, 1987), 19–22.

38 That is, the names al-ʿAlī (the Exalted) and al-ʿAẓīm (the Mighty).

39 A famous elliptical saying which means that when one is brought nigh (*muqarrab*) to God, one understands that one's previous good deeds, although good in themselves, were in fact impure, being polluted with subtle sins and vices, such as ostentation or ignorance.

40 Shihāb al-Dīn al-Suhrawardī (d.632/1235). A major Sufi of Baghdad, and author of the celebrated book *The Gifts of Gnoses* (*ʿAwārif al-Maʿārif*). He is not to be confused with several other Suhrawardīs, including the famous metaphysician of Aleppo.

41 The 'traces' (*āthār*) are the visible effects of the Divine Action in the physical world. No longer to perceive them is no longer to perceive them as autonomous realities, but to see through them to the unitary Divine Existence.

42 Literally, an 'arriver': a new spiritual condition. It may take the form of an inspiration [*ilhām*], beneficial involuntary thoughts [*khawāṭir*], external or internal knowledge, increase in zeal, or a condition such as Expansion, Contraction, Intoxication, or Sobriety.

43 Abu'l-Ḥasan al-Shādhilī (d.656/1258). A Ḥasanī sharīf, and the illustrious founder of the Shādhilī order.

44 *al-Dhahab al-Ibrīz fī khawāṣṣ al-Kitāb al-ʿAzīz*. This book appears never to have been printed, although a manuscript of it may be consulted in the Ẓāhirīya Library at Damascus (ʿĀmm, 8063).

45 Audition [*samāʿ*]: a sacred gathering in which there is teaching for the mind and heart through audible means, whether of Qur'ānic recitation, or the recitation of poetry with spiritual themes.

46 ʿAbdallāh ibn Abī Bakr al-ʿAydarūs (d.865/1461). A Ḥusaynī sayyid, the grandson of Imām ʿAbd al-Raḥmān al-Saqqāf. At birth his father gave him the title 'al-ʿAydarūs', meaning 'the Lion', in the expectation that as the lion was the king of beasts, so he would become king

of the Sufis. He lived to prove his father right, and died at the age of 54, and was buried in Tarīm. He is commonly known as 'al-ᶜAydarūs al-Akbar' (the elder).

47 The 'People' (*al-qawm*) are the Sufis, a name given to them as an echo of the *ḥadīth* which describes the circles of *dhikr*, which ends, 'They are the people whose companions shall never suffer misery.'

48 Al-Khalīl ibn Aḥmad was responsible for the first systematisation of the science of Arabic metrics.

49 *Uns*, or 'Intimate Comfort', is the opposite of *hayba*, or 'Awe'. *Uns* is higher than the station of *basṭ* (Expansion), which is in turn higher than *rajā'* (Hope). *Hayba* is higher than *qabḍ* (Constriction), which lies above *khawf* (Fear).

50 *Ghayba*, or 'Absence', is a corollary of 'Presence' (*ḥuḍūr*). It is to be unaware of the world, while *ḥuḍūr* is to be present with, and attentive to, God. Beyond them are Intoxication (*sukr*), and Sobriety (*sahw*).

51 *Sukr* is the condition of wayfarers drunk with the unveiling of the Divine Lights, while *sahw* is experienced by those who have reached their goal, and hence attained satiety.

52 *Jamᶜ*, or Union, is the opposite of *farq* (Separation). It is the alighting of Divine favours upon the heart, from the Lord to the servant, while *farq* is for the servant to maintain the courtesy of conduct and poverty in attitude appropriate to servitude. Beyond these are *jamᶜ al-jamᶜ* (the Union of the Union), which is *al-farq al-thānī* (the Second Separation): alternative terms for *baqā'*.

53 *Iḥyā' ᶜUlūm al-Dīn*, book 33.

54 ibid., book 8. For an English translation, see M. Abul Quasem, *The Recitation and Interpretation of the Qur'an: Al-Ghazali's Theory*. (Selangor, 1979 ce.)

55 Dhu'l-Nūn al-Miṣrī ('the Egyptian') (d.245/859). One of the early Sufis, he was of Nubian extraction.

56 There is a *ḥadīth* to the effect that those who die by drowning shall be considered martyrs.

57 Maᶜrūf al-Karkhī (d.200/816). Born of Christian parents, he accepted Islam at the hands of Imām ᶜAlī al-Riḍā, after which he became the disciple of Dawūd al-Ṭā'ī.

58 Cf. Qur'ān, 7:150, 14:8, 71:26.

59 Zayn al-ᶜĀbidīn ᶜAlī ibn ᶜAbdallāh al-ᶜAydarūs (d.1041/1631). The foremost scholar of his time, and a great Sufi of the ᶜAydarūs family of Ḥaḍramawt.

60 In a *ḥadīth* we read: 'The righteous dream-vision is one forty-sixth part of Prophecy.' (Narrated by Bukhārī, *Ṣaḥīḥ*, Taᶜbīr, 2.)

61 Abū Bakr ibn ᶜAbdallāh al-ᶜAydarūs (d.914/1508), called al-ᶜAdanī, since he moved from Tarīm to live at Aden. This epithet also serves to distinguish him from his father, al-ᶜAydarūs al-Akbar. He was

widely held to be the *quṭb* of his time, and was authorised by his father to form a teaching-circle of his own at the age of 14.

62 Man progresses towards God not through his own efforts – although these are usually a precondition – but through God's compassionate 'attraction' by which He draws him towards Him.

63 In other words, the spiritual states and stations conferred by God on His pure ones bear no relation to the 'dense' physical world of matter and dimension.

64 *Ilhām* is explained by Ḥabīb Aḥmad Mashhūr al-Ḥaddād as follows: 'The Divine states and conditions which come to man are various. There is a particular *wārid* for the *nafs*, and another for the *rūḥ*, and each has its own proper degree. *Ilhām* of the *nafs* manifests itself in the resolution of difficulties, the clarification of something not understood, or the dispelling of doubts: all these are matters pertaining to the *nafs*. The *nafs* seeks inspiration about what is correct, solutions to difficulties, and the lights of knowledges, through the subtleties it possesses. When the *nafs* rises up, the door of *ilhām* is opened, and this it receives by its own nature: *And the soul* [nafs], *and that which gives it proportion, and then inspires in it its wrong and its right* [91:7–8].' *Ilhām* in this context therefore refers to the *wārid* of the *nafs*, not that of the *rūḥ*.

65 *Hidāyat al-bayān* is the guidance a man receives from a Prophet or one of his representatives. *Hidāyat al-tawfīq* is the success that God gives a man in understanding and accepting *Hidāyat al-bayān*.

66 *Malakūt*: the invisible realm.

67 *Lāhūt*: the world of the Divine Names and Attributes.

68 *Fanā'*, which may be translated as 'annihilation' or 'extinction', is a term used to denote the disappearance of the soul's reprehensible attributes. At a higher level it denotes the loss of awareness of one's individual self in the face of the unveiling of the Divine Attributes.

69 God's Names and Attributes are divided into those of Majesty (*jalāl*) and those of Beauty (*jamāl*). To the first category belong names such as the Formidable (*al-ᶜAẓīm*), the Majestic (*al-Jalīl*), the Avenger (*al-Muntaqim*), the King (*al-Malik*), and the Slayer (*al-Mumīt*). The second category includes names such as the Merciful (*al-Raḥīm*), the Generous (*al-Karīm*), the Provider (*al-Razzāq*), and the Protector (*al-Ḥafīẓ*). There are also Names which are proper to the Essence, specifically: *Allāh*, the Unique (*al-Aḥad*), the One (*al-Wāḥid*), the Living (*al-Ḥayy*), the Real (*al-Ḥaqq*), and the Light (*al-Nūr*).

70 ᶜUmar ibn al-Fāriḍ (d.632/1235). Known as the 'Sultan of the Lovers', this Egyptian Sufi wrote symbolic poems of divine love and gnosis which are to this day immensely popular, and can be heard wherever there are Sufi gatherings. The lines cited here are from his *Dīwān* (ed. ᶜAbd al-Khāliq Maḥmūd, Cairo, 1984 [1404]), p.238.

71 Muḥammad ibn ʿAlī al-Sūdī (d.932/1526). A Yemeni scholar and Sufi who taught in the city of Taʿizz.

72 *Baqā'* ('Subsistence') is attained when the awareness of the world and the self return after extinction [*fanā'*]; but this awareness no longer comprises a veil between the servant and his Lord, for he continues to behold the theophanies [*tajallīyāt*] of the Truth.

73 Miracles which appear at the hands of God's pure ones; to be distinguished from *muʿjizāt*, which are miracles which appear through Prophets.

74 *God only desires to remove defilement from you, O People of the House, and to purify you thoroughly*. (33:33)

75 Abū Madyan al-Ghawth (d. 594/1198). Sufi disciple of the famous Abū Yaʿzā of Marrakesh. He is buried in Tlemcen. His own disciples included Ibn Ḥarāzim of Fez (d.633/1236), and ʿAbd al-Salām ibn Mashīsh (d.625/1228). The latter, before being killed by a remote Berber tribe he was calling to Islam, taught the great Abu'l-Ḥasan al-Shādhilī (d.656/1258). Al-Shādhilī, in turn, became the eponymous founder of the *Ṭarīqa Shādhiliyya*, which remains today one of the great religious orders of the Muslim world.

76 September 10, 1661.

INDEX